han

brutal beauty | hidden heritage **guide**

"*Dispirited by bickering and blatant architectures, the citizen rummages through the city looking for those sights and spaces that reflect a human scale. The citizen finds consolation in the neighbourhoods and unpretentious way stations, the abandoned, the undeveloped, the modest, looking for the town that seeks to be adopted before it capitulates to reality.*" (DiCicco, 2007)

hamilton

brutal beauty | hidden heritage **guide**

An alternative exploration guide to the City of Hamilton, Ontario.
by Ian Dunlop, University of Waterloo

A major research project in Local Economic Development
WATERLOO | ENVIRONMENT

Published by:

Hamilton, Ontario
www.strategicinterchange.ca

ISBN 978-1-894955-98-0

Preface

This Major Research Project was first conceived as a "Green Guide to Hamilton" to capitalize on the emergent urban green tourism trend. Having recently visited a number of cities across North America with my partner, it was clear that each of these cities have their own identity that has evolved over time based on their location, a unique urban structure, built heritage, and relationship to its surrounding region. From a local economic development perspective, it is important to understand a city's "place," in order to develop effective strategies for growth and vibrancy.

There is usually some form of publication available when visiting "rust belt" cities, promoting local tourism, built/industrial heritage, architecture, sustainability projects and alternative transportation. These publications identify and promote the unique places in the city that aren't the usual tourist spots, and offer an understanding of the history and context behind them.

In creating this book, I saw an opportunity to combine my professional expertise in mapping and design, past business experience in publishing, and urban planning, for my Masters research project in Local Economic Development. Also, my experience working in the Hamilton community arts scene, on initiatives such as rapid transit, on citizen committees and with the Chamber of Commerce has provided me with many insights on the city.

The project has taken me on a journey of discovery through the concepts of urban green tourism, sense of place, and understanding the challenging dichotomies present in Hamilton today. There is no shortage of ideas for what will make Hamilton a better place. But unfortunately there are clear divides between the opinions of central core urbanists, suburbanites and rural residents on the city's ailments and cures. The extremists in each group are equally unreasonable, for none of them works towards a vision of the whole city. Hopefully, this book will help expand those narrow views, and the views of people visiting the city as well.

Local residents and visitors alike may find this type of guidebook to Hamilton very useful in helping them see a side of the city they otherwise wouldn't consider. Since undertaking this project just over a year ago, a great deal has changed in Hamilton. New developments are taking place across the city, and I have already made several revisions to early drafts based on the positive changes taking place on almost a daily basis.

I would like to thank my advisor and review committee, Dr. Luna Khirfan, and Karen Hammond from the School of Planning, and Dr. Paul Parker from Geography/Local Economic Development for their input and advice on this project.

This book is dedicated to my partner, Brian, whose patience and support throughout this process has been my greatest source of strength and stability.

Ian Dunlop, University of Waterloo

www.hamiltour.ca

Introduction

People are looking for different kinds of travel experiences, whether just for a few hours, a day trip, or as part of a longer excursion. Local citizens should also be aware of the unique exploration opportunities that exist just beyond their own backyards. Increasingly, people desire experiences that are local, encompassing shopping, eating, learning, exploring, cultural awareness and awakening. This type of exploration is called "urban green tourism." Businesses are waking up to this new trend as well. Once overlooked areas are being revitalized as new residents and businesses move in, seeing the future value of investing there.

This book is a timely undertaking for Hamilton, as many cities are now promoting their sustainable development initiatives, renewal opportunities, established neighbourhoods, arts & culture, heritage, natural and environmental features, to visitors and residents alike. The book is also a personal exploration of the city, and I hope you enjoy reading it.

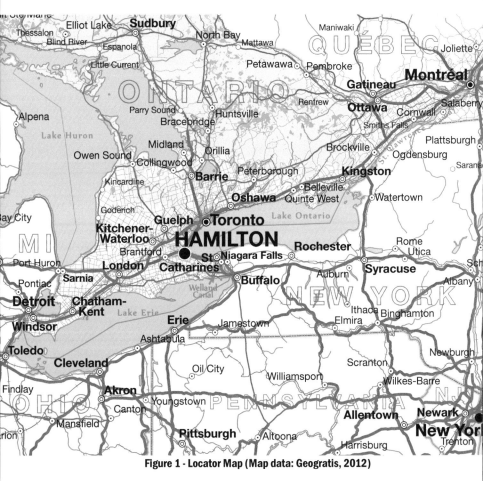

Figure 1 - Locator Map (Map data: Geogratis, 2012)

What is urban green tourism?

The concept of "urban green tourism" was seeded in Toronto in 1993, when a group of businesses, government and community organizations came together to form the Green Tourism Association. A report was prepared, for what was then Metropolitan Toronto, by consultants The Blackstone Corporation. The report defined urban green tourism as:

> ...travel and exploration within and around an urban area that offers visitors enjoyment and appreciation of the city's natural areas and cultural resources, while inspiring physically active, intellectually stimulating and socially interactive experiences; promotes the city's long-term ecological health by promoting walking, cycling, public transportation; promotes sustainable local economic and community development and vitality; celebrates local heritage and the arts; is accessible and equitable to all. *(Blackstone, 1996)*.

The authors of the report also suggest that the words "green", "sustainable" and even "healthy" are interchangeable in this context of urban tourism, thereby enabling the concept to encompass a broad range local discovery and contribute to personal and communal wellbeing. Through engagement in this emerging trend, there is a window of opportunity to generate a competitive advantage for the re-branding of post-industrial cities through tactful economic development and marketing strategies.

The mantra of urban green tourism suits the purpose for developing this book about Hamilton; it is a unique guide to the city that can be enjoyed by local residents and visitors. This book can also contribute to developing a cohesive identity for a city that has lacked one since its municipal structure was amalgamated 2001 into a single-tier municipality by the provincial government in 2001.

So, let's start with some background information about the city, to begin informing the context for this new guide. But first, here are some symbols that will be used in this book, to help you cross-reference the wealth of information available within it.

Symbols used in the book

Most of the photos in the book have a camera icon and reference number. The number corresponds to a passage in the text description and usually to a geographic location on an accompanying map.

Camera Icons: are colour-coded by section.

Number Icons: ❶ ❷ ❸ are used when a picture is referred to in the text.

Page Icons: 14 36 60 are used to identify the page number where you can find additional information or map for a topic being discussed in the text.

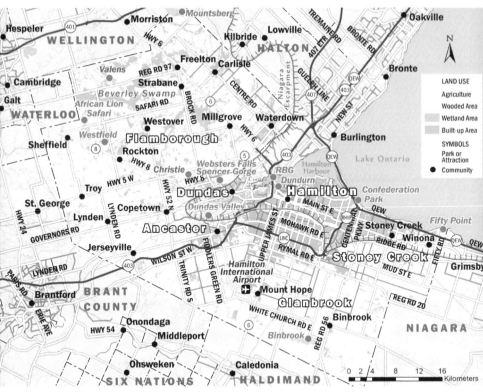

Figure 2 - Hamilton Area Map (Map data: Geobase 2012, LIO 2012)

Hamilton's community profile

Hamilton is a city of 520,000 (StatCan, 2012a) at the head of Lake Ontario, (see locator map on **2**, and area map on **4**). Hamilton developed due to the good fortune this location

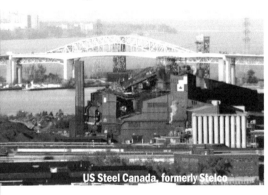

US Steel Canada, formerly Stelco

brought it, with a sheltered harbour **32**, rail **20** and road network **17**. Inexpensive hydro electric power from the Niagara area (Evans, 1970), earned Hamilton the moniker "The Electric City" (Gilbert 2006). Heavy industry eagerly located here, most notably steel manufacturing, employing 23,000 people in 1967 (Evans, 1970). By 1981, over a third of the city's total employment was in this sector, and Hamilton's steel mills produced 70% Canada's steel production (Jacobs, 2009).

In Pardon My Lunch Bucket (Proulx, 1972), a commemorative book published to celebrate the City's 125th trumpeting Canada's industrial powerhouse, saw no end in sight to the success for the **"Ambitious City"**.

Then, the 1981 recession and a prolonged strike at Stelco (photo below), then the city's largest steel manufacturer, followed in the 1990s by North American Free Trade (NAFTA) and increasing globalization, sent the city on a long, slow industrial decline. The result was a significant reduction in the industrial tax base and the loss of over 44,000 manufacturing jobs between 1981 and 2006 (Jacobs, 2009).

Abandoned auto plant, closed in the 1960s, was just recently torn down for new development.

The city's downtown and central residential neighbourhoods also reflected this economic decline. The city's deteriorating financial situation is often cited as the impetus for the provincially legislated amalgamation of the city with the five surrounding municipalities of the former Regional Municipality of Hamilton-Wentworth in 2001, to bol-

ster the local tax base (Arnott, 2008).

Nevertheless, Hamilton continues to produce most of Canada's domestic steel, albeit with a much smaller workforce, and has rebounded from economic downturns by continually expanding and diversifying employment within the region that now forms the amalgamated city. Figure 3 shows how employment across sectors have changed over the 20 year period between 1992 and

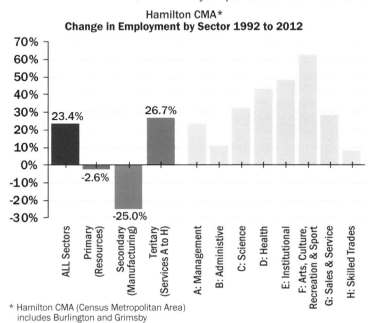

Hamilton CMA*
Change in Employment by Sector 1992 to 2012

* Hamilton CMA (Census Metropolitan Area) includes Burlington and Grimsby

Figure 3 - Change in Employment by Sector (StatsCan, 2012b)

5

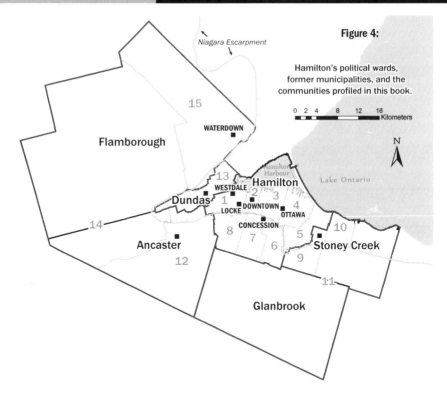

Figure 4:

Hamilton's political wards, former municipalities, and the communities profiled in this book.

0 2 4 8 12 16 Kilometers

N

Niagara Escarpment

15

WATERDOWN

Flamborough

13

Hamilton
Harbour

WESTDALE

Hamilton

Lake Ontario

Dundas

1

LOCKE

DOWNTOWN

4

OTTAWA

14

CONCESSION

8

7

6

5

10

Ancaster

12

Stoney Creek

9

11

Glanbrook

2012. In 1992, the manufacturing sector accounted for 10% of all local employment and now represents just 5% after a 25% decline over the period.

The decline is offset by continuous expansion in service sector, which has not only picked up the slack left behind by lost manufacturing jobs, but added nearly 90,000 jobs to the local economy. Arts, culture and recreation show the most dramatic increase, particularly since the turn of the century. A closer look at the annual numbers reveals this sector is volatile and was hard hit by the 1991 and 2008 economic recessions.

Hamilton's once booming commercial core, featured large multi-storey department stores Eaton's, Robinson's, Kresge, Woolworth, Zellers and the Right House **58**, along with all the major banks, jewelers and merchants of all manner, which succumbed to an unfortunate 1970's thrust of urban renewal "superblock" projects **44**, and simultaneous exodus to the suburbs. Nearby neighbourhoods, such as Beasley, now house some of the city's most challenged low income families, as is highlighted in a Hamilton Spectator series, "Code Red" (Buist, 2010).

However, recovery is taking place in the city's older neighbourhoods as a new generation of residents and small business entrepreneurs, attracted by low real estate prices, begin moving in and begin fixing up houses and storefronts. The Toronto

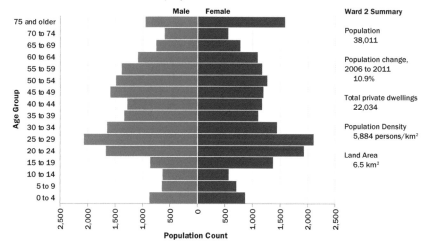

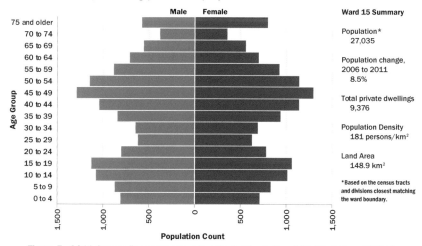

Figure 5 - 2011 Census Population by age cohort, Wards 2 and 15 (StatsCan, 2012c)

Star even noticed the trend in an article about the Friday night Art Crawls on James Street North **52** (Chapman, 2007). James is the north-south spine of the downtown's historic crossroads, King & James Streets. Galleries and studios open their doors to the public on the second Friday of each month, taking over a street that is on the road to recovery, and making it a place for people as it was years ago.

Citizens, artists, and small business start up such events through word of mouth and social media, which gain the recognition of the city administration and formal arts organizations as they become more popular, building vibrant neighbourhoods and commercial districts in the process.

The map in Figure 4 shows Hamilton's former municipal compo-

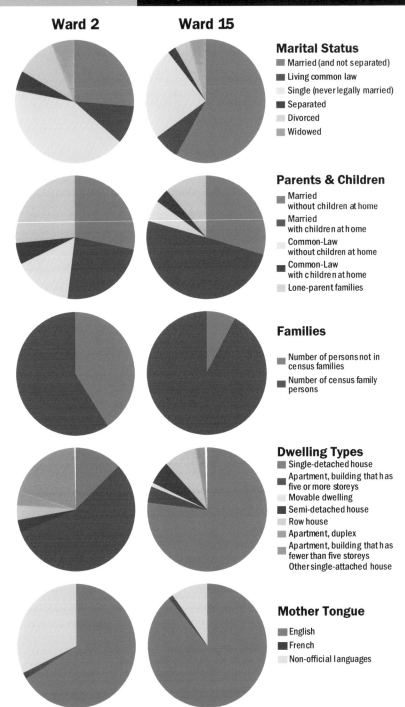

Ward 2   Ward 15

Marital Status
- Married (and not separated)
- Living common law
- Single (never legally married)
- Separated
- Divorced
- Widowed

Parents & Children
- Married
  without children at home
- Married
  with children at home
- Common-Law
  without children at home
- Common-Law
  with children at home
- Lone-parent families

Families
- Number of persons not in
  census families
- Number of census family
  persons

Dwelling Types
- Single-detached house
- Apartment, building that has
  five or more storeys
- Movable dwelling
- Semi-detached house
- Row house
- Apartment, duplex
- Apartment, building that has
  fewer than five storeys
  Other single-attached house

Mother Tongue
- English
- French
- Non-official languages

Figure 6 - 2011 Census Household characteristics, Wards 2 and 15 (StatsCan, 2012c)

8

sition, and the current political ward boundaries. To illustrate the dichotomy between the downtown and suburban/rural residents, a series of comparisons from the 2011 census are provided in Figure 5. Ward 2, downtown Hamilton, is comprised of the Beasley, Central, Durand, Corktown and North End neighbourhoods. Ward 15 is comprised of Waterdown , a rapidly growing suburban area, the eastern portion of rural Flamborough and hamlets like Carlisle and Millgrove.

Each Ward elects one member to city council. Although the downtown ward has a much higher population, Ward 15 covers an area over twenty times larger. The age cohort diagram illustrates the prevalence of the "baby boomer" generation and their families in Ward 15, while the downtown Ward 2 is home to a far greater proportion of the next generation of young adults. The pie charts in Figure 6, highlight the differences in personal relationships, family status, and common languages between these two areas. Ward 2 also has the highest population density in the city, with most residents living in high-rise apartment buildings, as compared to the prevalence of single-family dwellings in Ward 15.

The perception of high property taxes in the suburban and rural areas of Hamilton, where property values are highest, also keeps municipal amalgamation a hot topic for many residents of these areas, with groups like the Committee to Free Flamborough determined to break the former town away from the central city. Likewise, many

residents within the core areas of old Hamilton consider the amalgamated city's political ward system is not fair representation by population (McGreal, 2011).

"Us and them" attitudes between different parts the Hamilton have become prevalent over these and other issues, and are now often played out in social media. Different circumstance and ideologies bring about suspicion of motives for economic development and short-sighted goals, alongside conflicting opinions of what is best for the city. This conflict, which may be brought about by the differences in demographic and living circumstances highlighted above, underscore one of the challenges in building a cohesive **sense of place** to its citizenry. Tolerance is one of the 3T's neces-

Ghosts of the past linger throughout the city.

STINSON SCHOOL

Stinson Lofts condo conversion of an old school.

Dundurn Castle

economic circumstances that have brought Hamilton to where it is today, for better or worse, are continuing to forge its identity and have certainly instilled passion in its residents.

Alongside the unique character of the city's people and distinct communities stands an impressive built heritage, much of it dating back to the early 20th century. For example, the Pigott Building, Hamilton's first "skyscraper," was restored and turned into condominiums 39 (Arnott, 2008). The Lister Block, built in 1924, is another prime example of renewal. This 6 storey, terra cotta accented building, which boasted, the first indoor mall in Canada (Manson, 2011a), reopened, fully restored, in March 2012, after 20 years of being left to decay and neglect 37. The Royal Connaught Hotel, however, awaits its white knight 59. Hamilton's boom times brought these buildings to life, and the bust times ensured that not all of them were destroyed to make way for more modern skyscrapers. There have been many buildings lost, most significantly due to the Civic Square urban renewal developments of the 1960s and 70s 44. However, the remaining stock of late 19th and early 20th century downtown buildings in Hamilton is still impressive.

sary to attract the Creative Class, the others being Talent and Technology (Florida et al. 2009). Low-density suburbs, by their very nature, discourage tolerance because "we spend no time whatsoever in communion with our fellow citizens." (Kingwell, in Brown & Burns, 2006).

Tolerance starts with an understanding that there are different points of view, and we should not feel threatened by the expression of them. It works both ways; the creative class downtown must also be tolerant of middle class suburban opinion. Both need each other to make a successful city. Where once the suburbs were dependent on the central city for the region's vitality, the relationship is now one of "uneasy parity" (Rybczynski, 1995). The geographical, political and

The Niagara Escarpment, known locally as "The Mountain," cuts a dramatic path through the area and provides a backdrop for the city below, or a stunning view from the "upper" city above. The Bruce Trail and a number of city paths and bikeways crisscross the Mountain 24, which also connect a series of parks and conservation areas (Hamilton, 2011). In addition, over one hundred waterfalls spill over the edge of the Escarpment, which is classified as a United Nations World Biosphere 79. Waterfront parks on Lake Ontario, the western Harbour, and Cootes Paradise offer a broad range of recreational possibilities. Popular attractions include The Royal Botanical Gardens (RBG), Dundurn Castle, and the Warplane Heritage Museum at Hamilton International Airport (see map 4). Hamilton International is also Canada's largest inter-modal cargo airport 33 (HIA, 2011).

Hamilton also has a large rural area (see maps on 92-95), with vast areas of farmland, offering a wide variety of locally grown foods. Environmentally sensitive areas, such as the Beverley Swamp 82, and outdoor recreation opportunities abound. Nearby communities offer also offer their own unique cultural and heritage experiences, such as Six Nations of the Grand and Mississaugas of the New Credit First Nations, which are just south of the city. Toronto, Niagara Falls and the U.S. border are less than an hour away. There is a lot to say about Hamilton, how it developed, and what it has to offer to visitors, potential developers and its own residents.

The challenge is to break out of the established ways of thinking about the city. We must go beyond the City's vague strategic vision "To be the best place in Canada to raise a child, promote innovation, engage citizens and provide diverse economic opportunities." . Citizens need a vision they can rally around and become engaged in.

There is a tendency to treat places as objects rather than environments (Canter, 1977). The abstract notion of "the best place in Canada to raise a child [etc.]" is imposed independently of Hamilton's context—objectifying it rather than embracing the multi-faceted qualities of its environment. A better understanding of the diverse communities and challenges the city faces can lead to a more specific vision for the city.

The following list summarizes the current situation in Hamilton and informs some of the themes and topics to be expressed in this book, with the goal of promoting better understanding.

STRENGTHS
- Multi-modal transportation hub: Road, rail, seaport, 24-hour airport
- Strategic location
- Natural amenities: Escarpment, waterfalls, and two waterfronts
- Built heritage: Downtown buildings, infrastructure, community cores, renewal/reuse opportunities, heavy industry
- Rural area: Local food, agriculture, recreation, biodiversity
- Unique neighbourhoods, shopping districts and walkable streets.
- Economic and social diversity.

WEAKNESSES
- Sensitivity to economic downturn
- Negative perceptions of heavy industries,

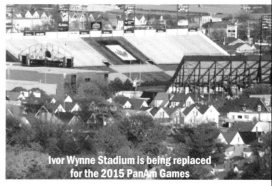

Ivor Wynne Stadium is being replaced for the 2015 PanAm Games

poverty, crime and safety, downtown in decline, high taxes
- Municipal amalgamation threatens community identity and autonomy
- Cynicism and negative attitudes
- Lack of cohesive identity
- Traffic and one-way "traffic sewers"
- Infrastructure deficit
- Inconsistent political leadership and direction
- Social service costs and provincial downloads burden property tax base

OPPORTUNITIES
- Regional and international trade hub
- Proximity to Toronto and U.S. Border
- Attractive property values
- Skilled, diverse workforce
- Growing arts and culture scene
- Downtown renewal
- Waterfront development and recreation
- Alternative transportation: LRT, cycling, one-way street conversion
- All-day GO Train service
- New stadium for 2015 PanAm Games

THREATS
- Loss of heritage features: Decay and neglect of older buildings
- Ageing population
- Climate change straining infrastructure
- Inner suburbs at risk of decline
- Competition from other medium sized cities: Kitchener-Waterloo, Burlington, London, Toronto suburbs and U.S. border cities.
- Traffic congestion on inter-regional highways (QEW/403)
- De-amalgamation/political uncertainty

Structure of the Book

The content and layout of this guide is informed by the unique situation Hamilton presents to us. To promote a city successfully requires an understanding of how the place came to be and the historical developments that have led to the place it is today.

Hamilton is built on the infrastructure that supports it; railways, roads, ports, power, water and sewer. These aspects of a city are often taken for granted and overlooked by residents and visitors alike, but what is interesting about Hamilton is how its infrastructure, and thereby its success, is shaped and influenced by the physical geography of its economically strategic location. This section sets the foundation, as good infrastructure should, for understanding and exploring the other parts of the city, starting with Downtown Hamilton.

Downtown has a rich built heritage from nineteenth century commercial walk-ups to modern glass and steel skyscrapers. After emerging from the superblock of the 1970s, Downtown is now entering a more sustainable phase. Old buildings are being restored rather than demolished, and the legacies of superblock plans and one-way streets are starting to be mitigated. Many investors, from small entrepreneurs to large developers, and new residents as well, are seeing the great value and potential of locating here.

Hamilton actually has many "downtowns," both within its old city limits and the amalgamated suburbs. The next section explores these walkable communities and the diversity of experiences they have to offer. Each description is accompanied by a detailed map and photos to get you started on your tour.

Sections on the Environment and Rural areas of Hamilton continue to take us on our tour outward from the core. The earlier sections of the book provide a context for the environmental remediation and preservation initiatives that are explored. The importance of agriculture to

Hamilton's economy is also highlighted, a "hidden heritage" often overshadowed by the city's industrial "brutal beauty."

The tagline "Brutal Beauty | Hidden Heritage" is being used to encompass the main themes of urban green tourism in the city. Brutal Beauty refers to the industrial landscape and infrastructure in harmony with the Niagara Escarpment, waterfronts and rural countryside. Hidden Heritage refers to the built and cultural history of the city, alongside the natural environment waiting to be rediscovered.

More precisely, this book is an exploration of the city for the enjoyment of residents and visitors, promoting sustainable local economic and community development in the amalgamated city.

If one simply starts thinking in less traditional ways about tourism, and dives into the local creative and cultural undercurrents, there is a lot going on here. Local residents can be a place's the most influential marketers if a desirable emotional connection and sense of ownership is established. This book is an important step in helping to discover Hamilton's true identity as it is today, shaped by its past and the former cities, towns, villages and townships that it now encompasses.

Hidden beneath its brutal beauty is the heritage that has made the city a unique and special place, enabling a resilient outlook and sustainable future. Hamilton may lack the flashy attractions of Toronto or Niagara Falls, yet this understated nature is what makes the city attractive to the people already here, and those seeking an alternative to the flashy experience.

There is a lot going on here, and many stories to tell.

infrastructure

See map on page 18-19 for photo locations identified by the green camera.

Hamilton's early development was brought by the good fortune of its location, with a sheltered harbour at a crossroads of First Nations trails. A rail, and road network, fanned out from the city by the mid 19th century (Evans, 1970). Abundant hydro electric power from the Niagara area, earned Hamilton the moniker "The Electric City" (Gilbert 2006). Heavy industry eagerly located here, most notably steel manufacturing (Evans, 1970).

This section reveals the many generations of infrastructure that helped shape the city, from road and rail, to public transport, to abundant electric power, and an outstanding water and sewer system. Hamilton's infrastructure is changing, as old rail lines become bicycle routes, transportation priorities are re-evaluated, and waste treatment is upgraded to recapture energy and meet stringent environmental standards.

❶ Hamilton Harbour receives ships from the Great Lakes and all over the world via the St. Lawrence Seaway. The Skyway Bridge keeps traffic moving on the QEW. (Photo: B. Montgomery)
❷ Railways and electricity are the backbones of local industry.
Below: Map of Hamilton as a strategic transport hub.

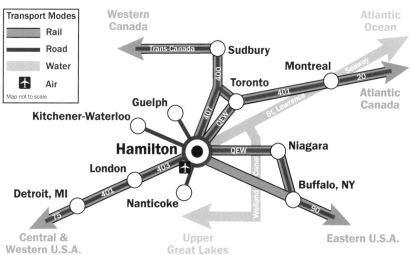

The High Level Bridge ❸ is part of the City's Western Gateway, project envisioned by Thomas McQuesten. The bridge provides a panoramic view of the west Harbour and Cootes Paradise; a much more picturesque vista than afforded by the present-day Skyway Bridge. McQuesten was also behind the construction of the Queen Elizabeth Way (QEW), Canada's first superhighway, in addition to grand greenspace plans such as Hamilton's Gage Park (Best, 1991). These large infrastructure projects came about as economic stimulus during the depths of the Great Depression, and continue to serve as vital transportation links and places for leisure and recreation.

Hamilton's International Airport at Mount Hope ❹ was originally a World War II training base (HIA, 2012; Evans, G., 2010), and has subsequently turned into Canada's busiest cargo airport ㉓.

While National Steel Car ❺, continues to produce rail freight cars, it once made locomotives for the Great Western Railway, and streetcars for local transit and radial railways ㉒㉓ (Disher and Smith, 2001)

There isn't much traffic on this Sunday under the Burlington Street Viaduct ❻, but this busy bi-level traffic artery connects the harbour's industrial district to the QEW.

From Trails to Freeways

As shown in the diagram on ⓯, highways radiate out as spokes from the Hamilton in all directions. The QEW was the first freeway, opening in 1938 (Stamp, 1987). Sections of the QEW, 403, Lincoln Alexander Parkway (Linc) and Red Hill Valley Parkway (RHVP) form a ring around the harbour and core area of the city (map on page ⓲⓳).

Critical to this link is the James N. Allen Burlington Bay Skyway Bridge (❶, and ⓯), which was completed in 1958 as a toll highway. Construction was prompted by the collision of a ship with the bascule bridge at the entrance to the harbour, and chronic traffic jams along the then two-lane section of the QEW (Stamp, 1987). The Skyway was twinned in 1985 to accommodate ever increasing traffic volumes. (Disher and Smith, 2001). Since then, the Linc and RHVP were built, which has further added to the QEW's traffic (see map ⓳). Controversial plans are under review to construct a new "Niagara to GTA" (NGTA) highway from Buffalo, around Hamilton, connecting to the 401 or 407 ⓹(NGTA, 2012).

❼ **Highway 403, approaching Main Street.**

❶ **The 2.2km long Skyway Bridge spans the Burlington Canal with a clearance height of over 36 m for ships to pass under** (Disher and Smith, 2001).

❽ **The Burlington Canal Lift Bridge is an engineering marvel, whether viewed close-up to see its impressive mechanical workings, or viewed in action as a ship passes between the lake and harbour.**

17

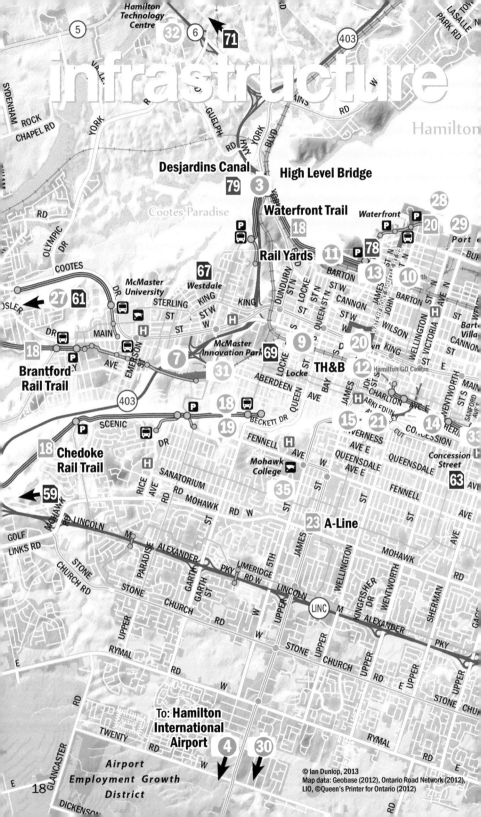

Railway Hub of Southern Ontario

Hamilton's location at the head of Lake Ontario and its natural harbour make it an ideal transportation hub. Highways and railways fan out from the city in all directions. Railways gave the harbour industrial areas direct access to Canadian and U.S. markets. Still today, although some of the rail lines are no longer in existence, rail transport remains a vital part of the city's economy.

The Great Western Railway (GWR) first forged this relationship in 1854, and nearly bankrupted the City. Ethics and conflict of interest rules not being what they are today, the limits of political and commercial relations were quite blurry and rarely called into question. No clearer example can be demonstrated than that of one of Hamilton's foremost politicans of the 19th century, Sir Alan MacNab, who lived in the finest estate in the city (Dundurn Castle) and was a major backer of the GWR.

MacNab's parliament changed the regulations preventing direct government subsidization of railroads and convinced the City of Hamilton to invest £50,000 in GWR stock. Originally, council agreed to £100,000, after threats the GWR would bypass the city in favour of Dundas, until it was pointed out that the entire assessed value of the

9 The TH&B tunnel under Hunter Street was built in 1895 to "avoid disruption to middle class west-end residential neighbourhoods" (Disher and Smith, 2001). The single-track poses a bottleneck for providing all-day GO Train service between Downtown Hamilton and Toronto. A new GO station will be built on the CN mainline in the North End, adjacent to the original Grand Trunk and CN station that closed in 1993 and is now LIUNA Station banquet hall (Manson, 2012b), **10**.

City's property was only £94,000. By 1864, hundreds of thousands of dollars worth of debentures had been purchased and almost 86% of City tax revenues went to service the rising debt load (Freemand and Hewitt, 1979). The rosier view of history is that MacNab brought the GWR to Hamilton, thereby building the City's industrial founda-tions (Evans, 1970).

If the railway had bypassed Hamilton, the city may not have developed quite the way it is today. But as its deep Harbour is well suited to large ships, development of the harbourfront industrial complex was inevitable, and the railways would follow. And follow the GWR did, with the Hamilton & Northwest, Hamilton-Port Dover, Hamilton & Lake Erie and Toronto, Hamilton and Buffalo railways coming in the following decades (Disher & Smith, 2001).

Passengers came on the railways, too. The GWR, later Canadian National (CN), and the Toronto, Hamilton & Buffalo Rly. (TH&B), later purchased by CP, both operated impressive stations. The art-deco TH&B station on Hunter Street ⑫ was refurbished in 1996 to become the new Hamilton GO Centre, with four trains per day to and from Toronto. The station is now also the inter-city bus termi-nal. The last trains left the Corinthian temple-styled CN station on James Street North ⑩ in 1993 (Manson, 2012b), as Via Rail and all-day GO train service did what MacNab once threatened the railways would, bypassing Hamilton in favour of the Aldershot station in Burlington.

⑬ **The Custom House built in 1860 is today the Workers Arts & Heritage Centre.**

⑪ **The original rail yards are now operated by CN. The yards are a barrier between the planned West Harbour community development and the waterfront. The yards are not likely to move anytime soon without government subsidy for relocation, which is what put the railway there in the first place. In Hamilton, the rails are forged of irony.**

21

Incline Railways

There were two incline railways in Hamilton in the early twentieth century. The Hamilton & Barton and Wentworth Street Incline Railways operated from about 1895 to 1936. Although the inclines could carry autos and small trucks, the increasing ease of travelling by road up the mountain sealed the fate of the inclines. The Hamilton & Barton incline was seized by the city for tax arrears, and later dismantled in 1943 for scrap during the wartime metal shortage.

14 The East End (Wentworth Street) Incline Railway, illuminated on a winter's night
(Photo: Local History & Archives Department, Hamilton Public Library) (See map **66**)

15 The Hamilton & Barton (James Street) Incline Railway.
The incline operated from 1895 to 1936. Some remnants remain such as a concrete retaining wall beside the Sherman Access.
(Historic Photos: Albertype Company/Library and Archives Canada).

Remains of a support footing for the Hamilton & Barton Incline Railway. The James Street Steps are in the background.

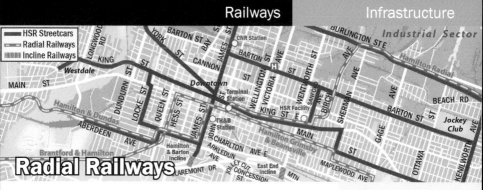

Radial Railways

The first radial line operated between Hamilton and Dundas in 1875, powered by small steam locomotives (Disher and Smith, 2001). But it was the advent of electric power brought about a revolution in local transportation. The first electric inter-urban railway line connecting Hamilton, Grimsby and Beamsville was first conceived as transport for bringing perishable fruits and vegetables quickly to market (Ibid.). The Grand Trunk purchased the railway due to its successful fruit transport business and extended the line. Power was originally generated by steam turbines heated from coal at a plant along the line in Stoney Creek .

Local businessman John Patterson realized that water power was superior to steam generation and could be produced in abundance thanks to the drop of the Niagara Escarpment. Patterson and his group of investors set up a new generating station at DeCew Falls, near St. Catharines in 1898. The Hamilton Street Railway became part of Patterson's company, Cataract Power, which soon held a monopoly on the local power supply (Evans, 1970).

The radial and streetcar network quickly expanded. The next radial was the Hamilton Radial Electric Railway, started by Patterson in contract with Siemens in 1894 (Disher and Smith, 2001). The line ran from Hamilton, along the beach strip to Burlington, Bronte and Oakville. Along with the beach, an amusement park located south of the Canal must have been a popular weekend getaway spot for weary citizens (Manson, 2002; Evans, G., 2005). Another line was built to Ancaster and Brantford. Buses and the Great Depression signalled the demise of the radials, the last of which ceased operation in 1931. The map at the top of the page shows the extent of the radial railways and Hamilton Street Railway streetcar routes, circa 1930.

16 The Powerhouse restaurant in downtown Stoney Creek was once a coal-fired steam electric generating station powering the Hamilton, Grimsby and Beamsville Railway.

However, by 1898, DeCew falls near St. Catharines, not Niagara Falls, was where most of Hamilton's electric power came from. Proximity to abundant, inexpensive electricity was critical in Hamilton's early industrial and transportation development (Evans, 1970).

Rails Become Trails   ⑰

⑱

⑰ The Escarpment Rail Trail crosses the Kenilworth Access providings a paved 6.4km cycle and recreation trail without any street intersections between Wentworth Street and Limeridge Road.

⑱ The Hamilton-Ancaster Radial Trail offers a gravelled 5.4km length without street intersections between Dundurn Street and Mohawk Road, including a Hwy. 403 overpass.

Hamilton is a city of bicycle freeways, thanks to the Niagara Escarpment and the railways that formerly served the area. Due to the legacy inherited by the City from a radial railway and two freight lines that were abandoned due to declining rail traffic, there are three major "rail trails" transcending the escarpment in Hamilton. Railways must use gentle grades to ascend steep inclines. The lack of friction between the iron wheels of the locomotives and the iron rails make railways an efficient mode of transport, but the same lack of friction is hazardous on steep inclines due to the increasing risk of slippage as the grade steepens. Fortunately for cyclists, these gentle grades now provide leisurely routes up the escarpment, from the central areas of city to the suburbs and beyond.

The **Hamilton-Ancaster Radial Trail** ⑱ follows the Brantford and Hamilton Electric Railway radial line, and continues as a regular signed route through Downtown Ancaster.

The **Escarpment Rail Trail** ⑰ follows the former Hamilton Port-Dover Railway and begins at Wentworth Street. Except for a short detour to circumvent the Lincoln Alexander Pkwy over a dedicated bridge, the route follows the original rail bed all the way to Caledonia.

The **Hamilton-Brantford Rail Trail** follows the western leg of the original Toronto, Hamilton & Buffalo (TH&B) railway, starting at the Aberdeen rail yards. The eastern leg of the TH&B, extending from the Aberdeen yard to Welland, remains an active part of the CP Rail network.

The **Lake Ontario Waterfront Trail** between Van Wagner's Beach and Burlington's Spencer Smith Park follows the original Hamilton & Northwestern Railway (Disher and Smith, 2001), and is another popular route for cyclists.
(See maps ⑱ and 92-95)

Mountain Steps

There are currently five sets of public stairs, or steps as they are more commonly referred, and one privately built staircase ascending the face of the Mountain (HPL, 2012). The Bruce Trail, several rough trails and unauthorized mountain bike paths also traverse the side of the escarpment. Most of the original wooden staircases have been replaced with metal ones.

The longest set are the stairs at Wentworth Street ⑭, with 498 steps built on the original site of the Wentworth Incline Railway (HPL, 2012). Some steps include a parallel bicycle trough allowing cyclists to escort their rides up or down the Mountain instead of carrying them. When viewed from the other side of the Harbour at night, the steps are clearly distinguishable from the mountain road accesses as vertical strings of light up the escarpment face.

Steps, like these ones connecting Dundurn Street to Garth Street ⑲, are well used by Hamiltonians, whether for fitness, recreation or practical transportation. The auto-oriented Mountain road accesses are inhospitable to pedestrians or cyclists.

⑮ **The Mountain View Motel awaited pedestrians at the top of the James Street incline and steps until razed in 1937. It featured a ground floor bar (no more steps to climb for the weary traveller), although prohibition curtailed the serving of alcoholic beverages in 1916** (Photo: Local History & Archives Department, Hamilton Public Library). **The site of the hotel is now Southam Park, and the outline of the hotel is marked by a stone platform overlooking the Claremont Access.**

The Railway Without Rails [20]

Inter-city transit services operate from the Hamilton GO Centre, at the TH&B railway station [12].

The Downtown hub of local HSR bus service is the new MacNab Transit Terminal, [20]. The new location eliminated on-street bus idling in the Gore Park precinct, which now opens up that area for pedestrian use [56]. The transit shelters and terminal building feature green roofs. The pavement is thermally heated in winter to prevent freezing (Hamilton, 2011a).

Transit service in Hamilton is provided by the **Hamilton Street Railway** (HSR). The HSR serves over 21 million passengers annually, with a fleet of 217 buses (CUTA, 2011). As the name suggests, public transit in Hamilton started with streetcars operating on rails. The first horse-drawn streetcars came into service in 1874, and the adult fare was just 5 cents (Manson, 2002, pp. 25). The streetcars were electrified in 1890, and Hamilton became known as "The Electric City" (Gilbert, 2006).

HSR streetcar service ended in 1951, replaced by electric trolley buses. The trolleys operated until 1992 along side a much larger fleet of diesel buses. The HSR was first to test pilot a new bus propulsion technology in 1985, compressed natural gas (CNG). A fleet of CNG buses soon replaced the electric trolleys, thanks to generous government subsidies at the time (Milner, 2009). Due to higher maintenance costs and lower reliability than diesel buses, and an end to the subsidies, the HSR's CNG fleet was gradually being phased out and replaced by hybrid-diesel technology. But recently the rising cost of diesel fuel, improved operating cost and efficiency of natural gas buses have spurred reconsideration. However, the greenest solution is the return of electric trolleys to the system. It is unfortunate that this infrastructure was removed.

For a quick getaway, the free Waterfront Shuttle service, Route 99, operates between downtown and the Hamilton Harbour waterfront from spring to fall. See map [18].

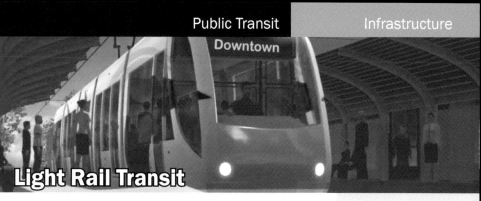

Light Rail Transit

Concepts for rapid transit in Hamilton can be traced back to the 1960's through the early 1980's, including monorails, and an "Intermediate Capacity Transit System" or ICTS, on which the Scarborough RT in Toronto and the SkyTrain in Vancouver are based (Hamilton, 2009a, citing Metro Canada, 1981). Due to an outcry over the project's cost and controversial routing, the plan was shelved.

In 2006, the Provincial Government created what was to be an arms-length agency to develop, fund and implement transportation solutions for Greater Toronto. This agency, Metrolinx, introduced "The Big Move" in 2008, an ambitions 25-year plan to develop a network of rapid transit routes across the Greater Toronto & Hamilton Area (GTHA). Included in this plan are two urban rapid transit lines in Hamilton, along with commuter GO Train service improvements (Metrolinx, 2008).

Hamilton's first proposed rapid transit route under this plan, the B-Line, is based on an already existing rush-hour bus rapid transit (BRT) route formerly called the Beeline, which began operating in 1989. The B-Line runs from McMaster University in the west, to Eastgate Square in the east, through the heart of Downtown Hamilton (see map 18). The corridor is already the HSR's busiest, and traverses the most densely populated areas of the city. The downtown and McMaster University are the biggest transit ridership draws in the city. The B-Line corridor is home to almost one quarter of the City's population, a density similar to that of Toronto, and its current bus routes accounts for one third of all transit boardings on the HSR system.

The HSR is also planning a new Crosstown BRT route using the city's expressway network to connect major hubs on the Mountain to the east and west ends of the City (Hamilton, 2010a).

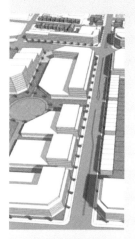

Above: Results of an urban design charrette envision the intensified mixed-use development potential for areas surrounding the proposed rapid transit stations (City of Hamilton, 2011b). **Over $1 billion in new transit-oriented development could evolve along the B-Line corridor in the next 20 to 30 years.**

Top: A simulation of the proposed B-Line LRT pulling into the Mary Street station in the International Village. (Adapted from City of Hamilton, 2011c)

Mountain Roads

Traversing the mountain by road has evolved from foot-paths originally used by First Nations to today's multi-lane freeways. The easiest paths were via the Dundas or Red Hill valleys, where the escarpment's cliffs are tempered by gently sloping elevations formed by floodways as the last ice age receded. These routes were densely forested and boggy (Manson, 2002). The more direct routes such as John Street, also originally a First Nations trail, were less muddy but very steep and difficult for wagons. By the mid 19th century, there were several mountain roads that were continually being improved. Tolls were charged to users for construction and maintenance of these mostly privately-operated roads (Evans, 1970).

The roads gradually came into public hands or were abandoned as more roads were built. James Jolley, for example, built his own mountain road, the Jolley Cut, to avoid paying the John St. toll and then donated the road to the city (Ibid.). By the early 20th century, there was a virtually continuous network of private and public roads traversing the escarpment across the city, as shown on the map and air-photo mashup at the top of the next page (Canada, 1934 and McFaul, 1943). The road patterns have changed over the past 50 years as population growth on the Mountain has increased traffic and the demand for wider, faster routes with shallow gradients. The John Street, Strongman's Road and Ottawa Street accesses are long gone, but rough trails still exist marking the sites of some of these original routes. Beckett Drive ㉔, James Mountain Road and Sherman Access ㉒ (formerly Mountain Boulevard) are original routes, and can be a thrilling car ride for the uninitiated.

The newest access is the Red Hill Valley Parkway (RHVP), a 5-lane freeway which opened in 2007 connecting Highway 403 and the QEW via the Lincoln Alexander Expressway. It is a controversial route, originally conceived in the

㉑ The 7-lane Claremont Access is one of four expressways scaling the Mountain. The Claremont was constructed in 1971 (Manson, 2002) amidst a building boom in the city. The steel retaining walls pinned to the side of the escarpment a necessary but visually displeasing feature.

The Jolley Cut, built a century earlier (Evans, 1970), seen crossing the bottom of ㉑ carries a higher daily vehicle volume of traffic (Van Dongen, 2011).

Location of Photo 24
Queen St.
Beckett Drive
Former mountain access roads
John Street
Strongman's Road

1950s (Spectator, 2007), which continues to incite passionate opinion in favour and against. Those in favour argue the route is essential to economic development, by opening up employment lands and eliminating congestion on local arterial routes. Critics point out the environmental costs of carving up a environmentally-sensitive river valley and forest that was the last remaining green space corridor between the escarpment and the lake in the urban area of the city.

A cross-town expressway parallel to Barton Street was also planned in the early 1960s, along with a "parkway" through the environmentally sensitive Dundas Valley. Fortunately neither of those plans were acted on.

An irony of modern transportation is that although technology continues to improve, roadways are built ever wider and longer to traverse steep inclines. Whereas older mountain accesses conformed to the landscape, contours and undulations of the mountain face, as shown in the map at the top of this page and 24, modern construction uses cut and fill to sculpt the landscape to build straight, flat roads. Instead of a natural mountain face, we look upon steel and concrete retaining walls (photo below), which are now failing with age. A better balance between efficient movement and environmental quality must surely be possible.

24 This intersection of Beckett Drive and Queen Street in this photo from around 1920 no longer exists (Photo: Albertype Co./ Library and Archives of Canada/PA-032649).

Rock slides and collapse are a regular and unpredictable occurrence. The Sherman Access 23 is periodically closed due to erosion under the roadbed (Van Dongen, 2011), and one lane of the Claremont Access remains closed due to failure of a 40-year-old steel retaining wall.

Water Works for Hamilton

Water and sewer systems are the lifeblood of the city, yet most residents take them for granted. Beneath the city streets is a vital network of sewers and water pipes. Hamilton's water treatment and distribution system was envisaged by one of Canada's leading engineers, T. C. Keefer of Montreal, after the city opened a competition following the outbreak of disease and increasing fire insurance rates due to the lack of a centralized water system (Disher & Smith, 2001). Keefer provided the city with different options for the new water system. The city wisely chose the Lake Ontario option, which would accommodate the city's future growth, even though it was the most expensive and the plant would be located well outside of the city limits at that time. The original route of the water main connecting the plant to the city can be identified between Main & Ottawa and Barton & Strathearne by a multi-use footpath carved diagonally across the street grid. (See maps, 18 and 73)

25 Remnants of Hamilton's early waterworks infrastructure can be spotted if you know where to look. This old standpipe of the Barton Reservoir is located beside the Escarpment Rail Trail. A footpath leads down into the rock bed of the now empty reservoir.

From this foundation, the city's waterworks and treatment facilities have continually expanded to serve the its current population and industries. The treatment plant currently operates at 77% capacity, and the next major expansion and upgrading of the system is set to occur in 2019 to ensure future growth demands are met. In the meantime, the City is investing $332 million to improve effluent quality as part of the Hamilton Harbour cleanup project 82 (Van Dongen, 2012).

24 The art deco interior of the water treatment plant. This hall is lined with water holding tanks on both sides.

Museum of Steam & Technology

By the mid 19th century, Hamilton was rapidly urbanizing, and the city's population more than tripled to 20,000 between 1846 and 1856 (Evans, 1970). Citizens drew water from private wells, which were easily contaminated. Cholera became so bad in 1854 that 1 in 40 residents died from the disease that year. The city sought a new public waterworks system drawing from the abundance of Lake Ontario, for both residential consumption and the expanding industrial sector (Hamilton, 2010c).

The Museum of Steam & Technology was the original pump house constructed for this purpose. It is the only surviving facility of its kind in North America, housing two 45-foot high, 70-ton steam engines. The engines pumped filtered water from the lake to large reservoirs along the side of the Escarpment, from which water was distributed by gravity feed to the city below. The museum is a National Historic Site and a Civil and Power Engineering Landmark. The engines were manufactured at Garthshore foundry ㉗ on Market St. in Dundas (see photo below). The engines operated in daily service until 1910, and on stand-by service until 1938 (Hamilton Civic Museums, 2011) as their function was gradually replaced by the massive water filtration and treatment complex that grew up around them to serve today's population and industries.

㉖ **Hamilton Museum of Steam & Technology, 700 Woodward Ave, is open for tours Tuesday to Sunday. Check website for hours of operation and rates.**

Hamilton Wastewater Treatment Facility is located adjacent to the museum at 500 Woodward Ave. Although access to the plant area is restricted, Globe Park, named for the methane gas storage painted as a globe ㉔, is a public greenspace with sportsfields and is home to the Hamilton Model Railroaders.

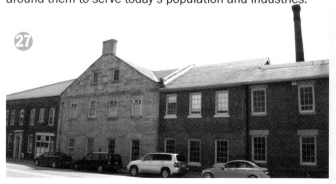

Canada's Busiest Great Lakes Port 🛟29

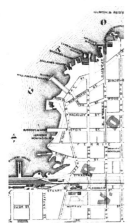

Map Above: Much of the port activity was concentrated in the west harbour in this 1882 map (Clark & Co., 1882)**. The area is now waterfront parks and marinas.**

🛟28 **The newest additions to the harbour's industrial skyline are the new Parrish & Heimbecker grain domes, each capable of holding nearly 30,000 tonnes of grain.** (Parrish and Heimbecker, 2012) **Beside the domes, a McKeil Marine tug** 🛟29 **awaits the call of duty in the harbour.**

The Port of Hamilton is operated by the Hamilton Port Authority under federal mandate. Landfilling has reduced the size of the harbour surface area by one-third since the 19th century. The map and air photo below (DEMR, 1934) show the 1934 shoreline and industrial development, and the infill that has occurred since, tinted in blue. The relationship between the City and the Port Authority has at times been adversarial. Scandals rocked the organizations in the 1970s, as shady real estate deals, dredging contracts and lack of infill regulation (Freeman & Hewitt, 1979) tainted the already murky waters of the harbour. But today, the harbour is Canada's busiest lake port, with new businesses, environmental remediation plans, and the impending release of Pier 8 to the city for planned waterfront development (Hamilton, 2012a) 🛟32. Unfortunately, most of the other industrial harbourfront lands are off limits to the public, although some good sightseeing is available by boat.

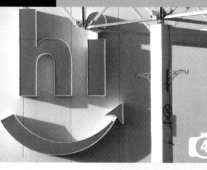

John C. Munro
hamilton international airport
Open 24hrs

Although Hamilton International Airport (HIA) ❹ handles 300,000 passengers per year through its international terminal (HIA, 2011), most of the airport's activity is centred on air cargo. HIA has no time-of-day curfew to limit its operations, unlike Toronto's Pearson Airport, so it has become a favourite of overnight couriers and grown to become Canada's largest inter-modal cargo airport (HIA, 2011). The airport is owned by the City and operated by Tradeport International Corp. under a long-term lease, who also operates Vancouver's international airport.

The area surrounding the airport is set aside for an ambitious industrial growth strategy. The total land area is 40% larger than the entire harbour industrial complex. The Airport Employment Growth District (map below) is envisioned as a transportation hub for businesses and green enterprises by 2030. While critics lament the loss of prime agricultural land to low-density trucking warehouses, the City maintains the importance of the district to future economic growth, as the remaining industrial land in the city is almost fully developed. However, for this amount of development to occur over the next two decades would be unprecedented, as will the city's $350 million infrastructure investment.

㉚ Photo Above: The Canadian Warplane Heritage Museum is located at Hamilton International Airport. Just look for the fighter jet!
(Photo: B. Montgomery)

The museum houses an impressive collection of vintage military aircraft, including one of the last flying Lancaster bombers in the world (photo below).

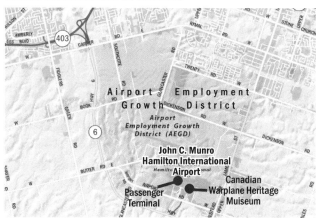

33

Infrastructure for Innovation 31

Hamilton has a history of innovation thanks to its industrial heritage. Steel manufacturing, and related industries like locomotives and rail car assembly, motor vehicles and farm equipment established a strong local economy and labour force. But as shown in the employment statistics in the introduction, steel and manufacturing play a diminishing role in Hamilton's diversified economy.

Over 18,000 new jobs in health and science sectors in were added in the past twenty years (StatsCan, 2012b). Hamilton's institutions are at the forefront of medical research and applied medicine. McMaster University Medical Centre 70 is a leading teaching hospital. The Juravinski Hospital 33 has a renowned cancer centre. And, McMaster is building a new health services campus in downtown Hamilton opposite City Hall 46 47.

From the early days of coal powered industry and locomotion, to green energy and high-tech, Hamilton's capability for resiliency and change is evident. But we must also learn from the mistakes of the past to avoid undesirable legacies.
(Historic photos: Library and Archives of Canada)

The Hamilton Technology Centre ㉜ opened in 1993 in Flamborough. This small business incubator provides start-up businesses with access to support and professional business advice they may not otherwise be able to afford or find on their own.

McMaster Innovation Park ㉛ is another high-tech business incubator, housed in a former household appliance factory. The next addition to this complex will be a state-of-the-art automotive research centre, associated with McMaster University.

270 Sherman ㉞ is a multi-use complex housing small businesses, craft industries and artist studios in a former cotton mill. A recent art exhibition held n the old factory's vast warehouse space (right), TH&B: "To Hell and Back" celebrated the work of local artisans with a historic nod to the TH&B railway that was once centred on Hamilton. Renwal efforts, like 270 Sherman, repurpose old factories and buildings for use as inexpensive studio and office space for artists and entrepreneurs to get started, with the advantages of a collective and collaborative environment.

Hamilton's post-secondary institutions, McMaster University and Mohawk College ㉟, both have outstanding reputations for entrepreneurship and innovation.

downtown

See map on page 42-43 for photo locations identified by the red camera.

I'm Still Standing

On Friday the 13th of April 2012, Hamilton's Lister Block was reopened after a $27 million renovation. There was much local fanfare, including live radio and television broadcasts, from the City's new Tourism office main floor of the building. Images from before the renovation show the dramatic transformation; from the damp and moldy carcass of the original shopping "arcade" to the brightly renewed ground-floor office and commercial spaces. Just a few years ago, the hulking 6 storey structure's broken windows and crumbling terra cotta details symbolized the long, slow decline and stagnation that had overcome downtown Hamilton since the early 1980s. The Lister's grand revival after 20 years of neglect and decay is a symbol of resilience and renewal for Downtown Hamilton.

This section presents some of the opportunities, and economic challenges, and development legacies present in Downtown Hamilton today. Renewal, redevelopment and resilience are not new to Downtown. The City is coming out of a dark age, so to speak, as developers and entrepreneurs see the value and potential available—if the timing is right. Downtown will never be the same again, it never was, nor should it ever be: Downtown is alive.

Photo at top:
A sign in a storefront window display in the Lister Block "I'm Still Standing" after the renewed building, at the corner of James Street North and King William Street ㉕ reopens. The Lister Block features a restored brick and terra cotta façade and an"Arcade" which was Hamilton's first indoor shopping mall. The photo at left shows the interior of the restored gound-floor Arcade.

37

King WIlliam Street, which is anchored by the Lister Block ②⑤, is also coming to life with a mix of cafes, restaurants, night life and the newly restored Lister Block as its western anchor ③⑦. The Dofasco Theatre Aquarius is home to Hamilton's only professional threatre group, and second largest venue in the city after Hamilton Place. The street has also been reconstructed with textured pavements and sidewalks to add to the pedestrian oriented activities.

The former Federal Building on Main Street ②⑥ is becoming part of a three-tower condominium hotel complex. The old building is being converted to premium condominium units. Original historic details such as friezes are being preserved.

A freight rail line used to run right through the city centre along Ferguson Avenue ⑤①. The rails are now gone, and in their place is a promenade featuring tributes to Hamilton's rich railway past, including a station pavilion at King Street used for community events and "makers' market" craft fairs.

The former inter-city bus terminal building at John and Rebecca Streets ②③ now houses a social services centre. Although the old bus bays are still present, it would be a very long wait to be picked up. Bus services were relocated to the Hamilton GO Centre ②⑥, which replace this outdated facility. The abandoned terminal is reflective of the vacant land and parking lots that could one day be redeveloped to new uses.

Repurposing old buildings is not a new thing to Hamilton—it has been happening for decades. Hamilton's first skyscraper, the Pigott Building ㊱, was converted from offices to residential units in the 1980s.

Once the City outgrew its majestic Public Libray on Main Street ㊵, adjacent to City Hall, the building was converted to provincial family courts. The main post office at Main and John was also renovated and converted to a courthouse in 1999.

The Landed Banking and Loan Building at Main & James Streets features very ornate detailing ㊶ and now houses a law firm.

The former Bank of Montreal at the southwest corner of Main and James Streets ㊸ is also now law offices, after briefly serving as a nightclub. (Photo: B. Montgomery)

Not every building can be saved, nor should it be. Restoration of old buildings is expensive, and can be more costly than tearing down and building new. Inexpensive suburban land lures sprawling development and the rise of the regional shopping mall, whereas earlier core-area buildings tended to be more compact, multi-storey structures on much smaller plots of land. Sometimes, these plots are also contaminated, due to the carefree industrial practices of old, and remediation to today's stringent requirements is very costly and time consuming.

Likewise, old buildings require expensive retrofitting to meet current ventilation, fire, communications and accessibility standards. As a result, prospective developers cannot always make the business case work even when government programs are in place to provide assistance—it simply isn't worth the bother when there is plenty of shovel-ready land elsewhere.

The Knitting Mills at Cannon and Mary Streets ⑭ is one such site, waiting in limbo for the right development environment and investment partnerships to solidify. There are promising signs of life, as the property was purchased by an equity partnership in 2011 and is currently undergoing feasibility assessment. There are many challenges, such as the high volume of one-way traffic passing by on Cannon, and the economic and social conditions in the immediate neighbourhood that could sink the marketability of the project (MacLeod, 2011).

Across the street, the offices of McCallum Sather Architects ⑨ provide a beacon of what can be done in the neighbourhood. Their own building has been retrofitted with green energy generation, appropriately emphasizing the firm's focus on LEED-certified and sustainable design projects (MSA, 2012) (Photo: B. Montgomery).

Few sites exemplify "hidden heritage" like the 19th century Amisfield mansion ㊼, hidden from street view and almost completely encompassed by the modern structures attached and surrounding it. At least the adulterated building is still standing and in use.

The wait for a saviour can be too long for some buildings to bear, and many have been lost to neglect, decay and eventual collapse. The Century Theatre suffered such a fate, as did the lobby building of the Tivoli Theatre. The Tivoli's grand main auditorium is intact **11** (Photo: B. Montgomery). The current owners, the Canadian Ballet Youth Ensemble, originally purchased the building for $1, but recently sold it in the hope that a developer will invest the over one million dollars needed restore the theatre and become their dream home.

It is not only old buildings where renewal opportunities exist. Hamilton's modern glass towers also have their share of vacancies **20 21 56**, although not in any imminent danger of collapse. Prime office space is available, and parking plentiful, to suit all types of ventures. Yet this surplus of commercial space can also make the business case of redeveloping old structures more challenging. Hence, the larger redevelopments, such as the Witton Lofts **1** and Stinson School tend to be residential condominium projects capitalizing on the trends toward sustainable urban lifestyles and Toronto commuters moving to the city attracted by the great value and GO Train service.

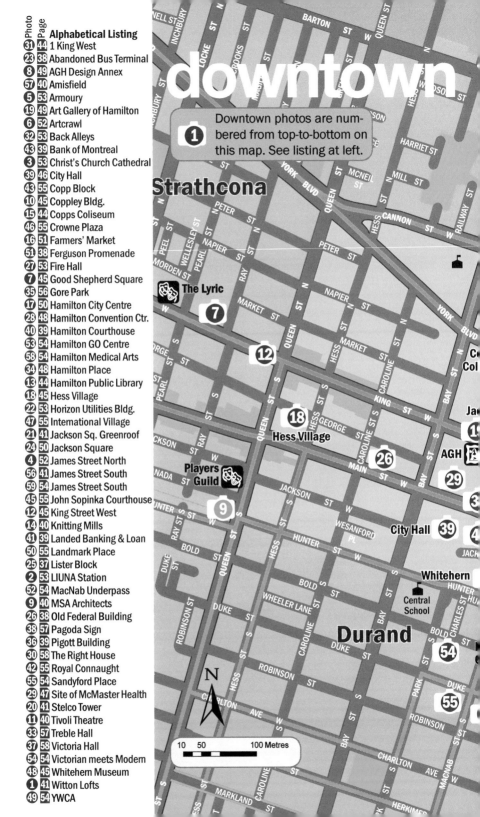

downtown

1 Downtown photos are numbered from top-to-bottom on this map. See listing at left.

Strathcona

The Lyric 7

12

18 Hess Village

26

Players Guild 9

City Hall 39

Whitehern

Central School

Durand

AGH 29

54

55

N

10 50 100 Metres

Mitigating the Superblocks

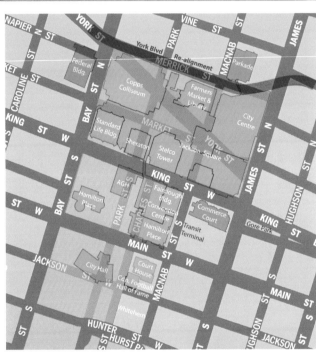

The Civic Square development area, at right in green, is superimposed over the original street network. The tinted streets no longer exist, and the close knit grid was irrevocably changed by the superblock developments starting with City Hall **39** in 1960 **46** (Freeman & Hewitt, 1979).

13 20 31 The buildings in this area are impressive and exhibit unique architectural features. The rooftop park **15** was less successful **50** and is little used.

... and one-way streets ⑫

The difference between King Street East and West ⑫ is more than just a directional distinction. On either side of James Street, which is the threshold between East and West, the character of Downtown Hamilton's major thoroughfare changes dramatically from century buildings and Gore Park on the East, to "Civic Square" on the West, a canyon of glass, steel, concrete and brick. The area is certainly not lifeless, as the sidewalks are busy with pedestrians, thanks to the new bus terminal 26, and the street filled with cars. Yet there is something about the high-paced bustle and sterile building façades that detaches people from truly connecting their environment and each other. This stretch of King Street, between York and Bay Streets is exceptional in Downtown Hamilton, although it hasn't always been this way (see map, 44).

However, new developments are reshaping the western side of Downtown, such as new hotels and condominiums along Main Street, a McMaster medical campus 47, and a revamped Art Gallery 49. A little further west, Good Shepherd Square ❼ is redefining what a superblock can be with a new mixed-income, inter-generational residential community with support services, integrated into its surroundings.

Photo Above: The entire downtown area is free wi-fi hotspot, although it will soon be obsolete.

⑫ **King Street (pictured) and Main Street are commonly referred to as "traffic sewers" due to the waves one-way traffic flow.**

⑩ **Some lovely neighbouhoods, streetscapes and buildings exist in the west end of Downtown, such as Hess Village ⑱, the new Good Shepherd Square ❼ development, and Whitehern 48, the former home of the McQuesten family, is now a museum.**

The Rise and Fall of Marbled Walls   39

Above: Hamilton's old City Hall was located on James Street North at York Street. It was torn down in 1960 to make way for an expansion of the adjacent Eaton's department store.
(Freeman & Hewitt, 1979; Photo: Stanley Mills & Co. Ltd./Library and Archives Canada/ PA-032617)

Right: The tile mosaics are a unique heritage feature of the current City Hall, which were carefully preserved through the recent renovations.

Hamilton's City Hall 39 on Main Street West was the beginning of Civic Square, which transformed a large portion of downtown Hamilton's streetscape from 19th century shops, businesses and walk-up apartments. "Shabby buildings and parking lots were cleared to make way for a new library, art gallery, theatre-auditorium, hotels, office towers and shopping malls coordinated with broad open areas and promenades" (Evans, 1970). Many North American cities undertook similar downtown renewal projects through this era, whereby blocks of lively store fronts were bulldozed and pedestrians segregated into climate controlled mazes without daylight as cars ruled the one-way streets outside. For a time it worked, but the gradual exodus of major retailers and employment to the suburbs brought a heavy toll from under which downtown Hamilton is re-emerging.

City Hall underwent major renovations between 2008 and 2010 to modernize its internal systems and improve energy efficiency (Hamilton, 2009b). The building was originally designed by the City's own staff architect, Stanley Roscoe, in the modern, International Style that reflected Hamilton's mid 20th century prosperity and forward vision for the Ambitious City. The most controversial aspect of the design was the white marble cladding on the exterior, which were substituted with concrete panels during the renovations due to the high cost of replacement in today's allegedly less prosperous times.

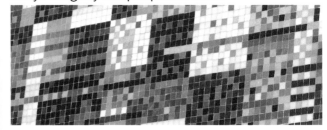

Boarded-Up

June 18, 2012 was moving day at the Hamilton District Board of Education building ㉙.

The board is consolidating their administrative staff at a new suburban campus, located near Lime Ridge Mall and the Lincoln Alexander Parkway. The school board outgrew their 1967 building and have operations spread across the city. The original construction of the building included a foundation for an expansion of the existing office tower (Freeman & Hewitt, 1979), but the Board seemed intent on new development outside the city's core. The plan is better aligned to provincially-mandated funding guidelines under which the board must operate. These same guidelines mean several inner city schools will close over the next 3 years due to declining enrolment. Is this development regressive or progressive for the city?

The site of the current building is to become a new health care research centre for McMaster University. It will be a mixed-use development making more intensive use of the property, half of which is currently a surface parking lot. Across the street, a new hotel and residential condominium complex is taking shape. Proponents argue the new development will bring economic spin-offs and more people to the core while critics lament the jobs relocated to the suburbs and loss of an iconic building as a zero-sum game. While the move and closures may make sense under the peculiar financial conditions dictated by provincial funding formulas, such policies limit local community development planning to a short-term view.

The Hamilton District Board of Education building at 100 Main St. W. was completed in 1966. Called a "style fake" or conversely a "respite from the 20th century urban style that dominates everything built downtown in the last 50 years" (Turkstra, 2012)**, the building is history nonetheless.**

The parking lot beside the building is visioned as mixed condo development, but a necessary severance application was withdrawn at the last minute.

Concrete Culture and Brick Bureaucracy

Above: The façade of Hamilton Place undergoes rebar rehabilitation work in summer 2012.

The unique structure of Hamilton Place 34 is a distinctive feature along Main West, fronted by the Irving Zucker Sculpture Garden that adjoins the Art Gallery. The brick-faced Ellen Fairclough Building is seen in the background.

Hamilton Place 34 opened in 1973 and has since hosted performances from a range of local to international artists (Betts, 2012). The impressive concrete structure and modernist auditorium are further examples of the city's brutal beauty, from both architectural and cultural perspectives. The adjacent Hamilton Convention Centre is housed on the lower floors of the Ellen Fairclough Building 28, and provides a variety of meeting rooms and a large trade show space. The facility is operated by Hamilton Entertainment and Convention Facilities Inc. (HECFI), an arms-length operating division of the City of Hamilton, which also owns and operates Hamilton Place and Copps Coliseum. The city has transferred operation of these facilities to private companies to eliminate their operating subsidy.

The Ellen Fairclough Building 28, which is also the home of the Provincial Government offices for the city, exemplifies poor 1970's planning and street integration (below). The narrowest and least pedestrian friendly sidewalks to be found in the downtown core are here. A redesign of the building accesses, opening up the sidewalk with integrated street parking through the removal of one traffic lane would greatly improve this canyon-like stretch of King.

Cultural Annexation ⑧

The Art Gallery of Hamilton (AGH) ⑲, established in 1914, is one of Ontario's largest galleries with a collection of over 9,500 works (AGH. 2012). For some time, the Art Gallery of Hamilton was disconnected from the community it served. As the city struggled with its own cultural identity, so too did the gallery in its fortress-like structure atop a parking garage built in 1977. Thanks to an award-winning redesign completed in 2005, the AGH is now lively reflection of a local arts renaissance, offering an eclectic mix of contemporary and traditional works. It is a treasure being rediscovered by the community. Admission to Gallery level two is free. Check the AGH website for hours of operation, fees, exhibit and event information.

The AGH's Design Annex ⑧ recently opened on James Street North in the City's up-and-coming arts district. The new storefront offers funky home decor, the works of local artists and becomes a lively part of the monthly Art Crawl scene. Accessibility and visibility of art in its many forms is a sign of the cultural awakening happening in Hamilton, and it is good to see the more formal outlets like the AGH to come along side the informal arts venues of the City's independent galleries and studios.

Above: The AGH letters stand high over King Street as its building strives to get noticed behind the imposing and little-used pedestrian overpass connecting Jackson Square and the Convention Centre.

Although the AGH is an important cultural institution today, its site and the area around it was once a walkable neighbourhood of shops, businesses and residential flats. The aerial view at left highlights what was demolished to make way for Civic Square (see map 44).

Best Intentions of the Time ㉔

A stunning forty-four acres of downtown core was demolished from the 1960s to 1970s to make way for the Civic Square urban renewal project that was believed would ensure the economic vitality of Downtown Hamilton for decades to come. The Lloyd D. Jackson Square, named after a former mayor of the city, is the centre piece, featuring 4 office blocks, thousands of square feet of retail space, and underground parking, topped by an under-utilized rooftop pedestrian promenade intended to provide public greenspace in the heart of the city ㉔. The Hamilton City Centre ⑰, formerly the Eaton Centre, was the last addition of retail space to the "superblock" that was once filled with nineteenth and early twentieth century storefronts and residential flats. The new development could not stem the tide of downtown decline; a situation repeated in other industrial cities across North America ㊾.

Many of the original stores are gone. Jackson Square and the City Centre went through difficult times, but signs of rebound are apparent. A new generation of ethnically and culturally diverse shops are appearing alongside some of the more familiar retail chains, exemplifying the increasing diversity of people living in and around the central part of the city. Jackson Square was an exercise in Project-based Planning, widely popular at the time of its conception, where a project must be big to be meaningful; so big as to overwhelm and alter what already exists (Gratz & Mintz, 1998).

Above: A ghost from the past? A broken Eaton's sign still remains affixed to City Centre ⑰.

㉔ The little-used public open space atop Jackson Square is an early "green roof".

⑰ To preserve the symmetry of the interior of the City Centre the main entrance off James Street is located south of the Rebecca Street intersection, not of opposite it. The dead end of a false façade is the unfortunate result of poor context-sensitive design.

Public Markets: "Buy Local" Starts Here 16

The Hamilton Farmers' Market 16 was originally an open-air market at the corner of York & James Streets. The Market moved to its current indoor location in 1980. It was formerly housed in a dingy parking garage beside the former Eaton's department store after construction of Jackson Square. The facility was renovated and reopened in 2011, featuring new community kitchen facilities and etched glass façade with doors enabling the market to spill out on to York Boulevard in fair weather. Unfortunately there are few other street front businesses in the immediate area to make the market a vibrant destination in the core.

Downtown markets can generate several times the gross sales per square foot of space than shopping mall stores (Gratz & Mintz, 1998). The Hamilton Market stalls are crammed full of goods for sale, and alive with people purchasing, browsing and selling. As the city looks to the success of its business incubators and accelerators that nurture new small entrepreneurs, it should not overlook the locally-grown businesses that can thrive if given the right opportunity through a local market as part of its economic development strategy. The market provides many spin-off benefits by of supporting all creative entrepreneurs and local agricultural sector. Markets support the local economy by recirculating dollars spent within the community, in a shopping environment that bridges the gap between rich and poor, old and young and cross-cultural barriers. "At markets, shopping is an event, not a chore," (Gratz & Mintz, 1998, p. 212).

Above: The Birks Clock once adorned the southeast corner of James and King opposite Gore Park **56**. The historic clock was refurbished and now resides inside the Farmers' Market **16** safe from outside elements. The jousting knights provide hourly performances.

Photo at left: The Hamilton Farmers' Market as it was in the early 20th century. (Albertype Company/Library and Archives Canada/ PA-032890)

Heritage, Arts and Culture

Buildings along James Street North are being purchased and refitted to become artist studios and eclectic storefronts offering art, handmade crafts, furniture and home decor from rustic to chic. The street comes alive the second Friday of each month for Art Crawl, when studios, galleries and shops keep their doors open late. The opportunity is to mix and mingle, see and be seen and provide a venue for local artists to show their work with pride. The street is closed to motor vehicles for two annual festivals, Supercrawl and Open Streets, which draw people from all over the city.

4 Advertisements on the sides of buildings become revealed when adjacent buildings are torn down. Ghosts from the past appear, sometimes for businesses long gone, or for ones that are still relevant today.

6 Monthly Art Crawls and the annual Supercrawl are a time to celebrate the artisans and creative community that is helping bring Downtown back to life, with James North as its focal point. (Photos: B. Montgomery)

The creative awakening of the street happens alongside traditional activities of this historically portugese-italian neighbourhood, featuring grocery stores with fresh produce displayed along the sidewalk, plus restaurants, bars and community halls. But there is a cultural shift occurring. A high proportion of the population in this area is between ages of 20 and 40, whereas the demographic trends **7** for suburban Hamilton shows a clearer "baby boom" population cohort and proportionally more school-

Raising values ㉒

aged children (StatCan, 2012). Statistics Canada confirm the broad age ethnic and income mix in the area, which is reflected in the range of building types, businesses activities and sense of community building here. Property values are also increasing quickly as the value and amenities of living are being realized. Assessment increases are more than double the average increase across the city (City of Hamilton, Teranet Inc., 2012).

The promise of a new GO Train station coming to James North, with all-day service to and from Toronto, is also attracting the interest of Toronto commuters. While the area offers better value than Toronto, yet with a similar urban lifestyle and amenities, there is the concern of gentrification and potential for lower-income residents to be pushed out. The Beasley (see downtown map, ㊸) neighbourhood, to the east of James, is one of the most socially and economically challenged in the city, with the highest poverty rate. As new people move in and fix-up houses and storefronts, the neighbourhood is being transformed. The changes appear to be positive, but will problems appear elsewhere?

㉒ **The Art Deco Horison Utilities building at John and Rebecca. Horizon is taking a lead role in energy conservation in the City through various programs and spearheading the City's energy mapping initiative.**

Left: **A walk through the north end of Downtown reveals a variety of architectural gems, from public institutions like the Armoury ❺ and Fire Hall ㉗, to historic churches ❸ and the former train station ❷, now LIUNA Station banquet and meeting hall.** (Photos: B. Montgomery)

Mobility, Living and Healing ⑤②

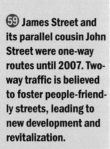

Old and new exist side-by-side in the varied developments between Main Street and the Mountain. Whereas Downtown west succumbed to the brutality of the bulldozer, and north has remained in a stasis until recently, the south has developed in a more haphazard fashion, with century old buildings butted up against modern high-rise apartment blocks. The neighbourhoods of Durand and Corktown (see downtown map, **44 45**) are worth exploring on foot, to appreciate the diversity of the architecture and the close-knit feel of the communities. Durand also has the highest population density in the city. Queen, James, John and Wellington Streets are each major corridors from the "lower city" to the mountain. The city's commuter bus terminal and train station ⑤③ is a focal point for mobility **26**.

⑤② **The murals within the pedestrian tunnel under the former TH&B Railway tracks at MacNab St. promote the city and its identity.**

⑤⑨ **James Street and its parallel cousin John Street were one-way routes until 2007. Two-way traffic is believed to foster people-friendly streets, leading to new development and revitalization.**

④⑨ ⑤④ ⑤⑤ ⑤⑧ **The broad variety of architecture and contexts one can discover within short walking distance.**

Opportunities, Large and Small

Heading east from the Gore Park area, known as the "Gore Precinct" ❸❺❻ one encounters the International Village, centred at King Street & Ferguson Ave. ❺❶ A mix of old three and four storey commercial/residential buildings, with newer developments like the Crowne Plaza hotel, house a variety of businesses, restaurants and services. This one-way stretch of King Street is just two lanes wide, compared with five lanes west of James, which along with the varied mid-rise buildings provides a much more relaxed and human-scale atmosphere to King. Main Street is a somewhat less comfortable place, with a discontinuous streetscape of old and new buildings broken by parking lots. The buildings are distinctive nonetheless, including the city's tallest and most recognizable skyscraper ❺⓪.

❸ **Ferguson Street promenade** ❸❽(Photo: B. Montgomery).

❺⓪ **Hamilton's tallest and most distinctive building (from a distance), Landmark Place stands 56 storeys—taller than the escarpment.**

Leaving Gore Park, at King and James one encounters thriving businesses, some ironic boarded up storefronts at the Royal Connaught ❹❷, historic fascades and contemporary buildings contributing to Downtown's variety ❹❸❹❺❹❻❹❼.

Parks are for People 35

35 The iron fountain is a centrepiece of Gore Park and was first erected in 1860 to commemorate the city's new municipal water supply 30 (Hamilton, 2010c).

Map at right: The Gore Precinct is highlighted on this map from 1882 (Clark & Co., 1882). **Based on the number of banks fronting on to the park and adjacent area, the importance of this area as a focal point for early commerce in the city is evident.**

Since the early 19th century, Gore Park 35 has been the central focal point of Downtown Hamilton. This three block island between the north and south leg of king has seen many changes over the years. This oddly-shaped "gore of land" started out as a muddy dump, with parts owned separately by city forefathers George Hamilton and Nathaniel Hughson (HPL, 2012). The city gained possession of the land by mid-century.

Initiatives to change or redevelop the park have been staunchly resisted, to the point where City Council had to order the demolition of partially constructed pavilions in the early 1980s due to public outcry. The iron fence along the north side of the park remains, separating people from the busy 5-lanes of King Street traffic. But in 2012, the south leg of King Street was transformed from a bus terminal to a pedestrian precinct. Buses were moved to a new, state-of-the-art terminal two blocks west on MacNab Street. As part of the City's Gore Master Plan, the south leg of King will feature a sidewalk promenade with restaurants and cafes. For now, the city's popular food trucks descend on the precinct to service the crowds eager to take back the street from the buses and cars.

build ings, vacant
City to other build
Renewal with a side of Chop Suey

Although the building cost just $735,000 to purchase, the final tally including restoration costs of Treble Hall ㉝, on John north of King, are estimated at over $2 million (Renew Hamilton, 2012). Such is the challenge facing developers in justifying whether to restore or rebuild. In the case of the Lister ㊲ the municipal and provincial governments contributed to the projects to make it work. But governments cannot afford to subsidize every project, and in an uncertain real estate market, the risks involved can make it difficult to find willing private investors. Fortunately, Treble Hall has found a saviour.

The condition the buildings are found in is also a determining factor in whether or not they can be included in redevelopment plans. On the south side of the Gore Precinct, between James and Hughson Streets, the prognosis is not as positive for the some of the buildings dating back as far as the 1840s. The developer, who has a proven track record of restoration through projects like the Landed Savings and Loan ㊶ and Bank of Montreal ㊸㊴ is proposing a redevelopment of the block that will see some of the existing buildings lost. But on the upside, the proposal is one of the largest block developments the Downtown has seen in recent memory. If the past cannot be saved, hopefully it can be learned from.

㊳ If the Pagoda sign were taken down, it could not be reinstalled due to modern sign by-laws. Therefore it will be restored in-situ.

㉝ A creative way to board-up windows was used on Treble Hall. The reawakening building began to speak to the city once again after years of neglect and silence. (Photos: B. Montgomery)

The right time and The Right House

The Gore Precinct is flanked by a variety of commercial buildings spanning over a century of city evolution from the late 19th to late 20th century. Prime examples are Victoria Hall ③⓪ was recognized as a national historic site in 1995 for its rare, hand-crafted sheet metal façade (Canadian Register of Historic Places, 2012). The Right House ③⑦ was Hamilton's first full service department store. Although now used as offices, it is last remaining building of its kind in the city.

The resilience story in Hamilton is ongoing. A symbol of decay looms over the eastern end of the Gore Precinct—the Royal Connaught Hotel ④② —once the swankiest accommodations and entertainment spot in the city. After several failed proposals for redevelopment as a mix of hotel, residential condominium, and commercial uses, it remains dark. There is more work to be done in renewing Hamilton, and it will be continuous.

For every new symbol of resilience accomplished, another symbol of decline will call out for action.

③⑦ **Victoria Hall**

③⓪ **The Right House**

④② **The grand entrance stonework retains a regal elegance, although the awning is now a rusting metal skeleton atop boarded-up store fronts.**

Royal Connaught ④②

Context, time and place

Hamilton is moving in the right direction, with many local actors on board and programs in place to move resilience effort along the right path. Resilience is challenging and it requires strong civic leadership to move the effort forward. Leadership in the form of political, community (social capital), and labour (human capital).

Hamilton's downtown problems are not unique, as North American regions have matured into a post-Fordist reality. The best laid plans for renewal and revitalizationn of downtowns can be quickly set aside by changing economic conditions and development elsewhere in the city. By example, Downtown Rochester, New York faced a similar situation. Rochester also had a downtown development similar to Jackson Square called Midtown Plaza—the first downtown urban mall in America, which included two department stores, office space and a hotel (Tumber, 2012). After a large suburban mall opened in 1982, Midtown became "increasingly seedy," the major stores pulled out and the complex was torn down in 2008 leading a "gaping hole in downtown Rochester's landscape." (Ibid, p. 57)

Hamilton has fared somewhat better. Jackson Square opened to much fanfare in 1972 (Wilson, 2012), with Eaton's as its anchor. Four other department stores remained in the downtown core. Hamilton's largest suburban shopping mall, Lime Ridge Mall, opened in 1981. The downtown department stores closed in the succeeding years, with Eatons finally closed its doors in 1997 (Noble, et al, 1999). Jackson Square went through a seedy period, but is not currently at risk of being torn down. It is emerging as a more vibrant destination for downtown workers and residents, as evidenced by the recent announcement of a new grocery store soon to be opened, in lock-step with the revival occurring throughout Downtown Hamilton.

After a major building boom through the 1960s and 70s, Hamilton's downtown skyline, viewed from a distance, has changed little. During that era, Hamilton's iconic City Hall went up, and has since been renovated rather than torn down as its predecessor had once it became outgrown.

59

communities

Hamilton: A City of Many Communities greets visitors on roadsigns as they enter the rural periphery of the City. The statement is indeed factual, but not one in itself to instill a sense of unified community of communities. Each part of the City is distinct, having at some point been separated from each other and gradually amalgamated through successive annexations and provincial amalgamation schemes. The suburban communities of Ancaster, Dundas, Stoney Creek and Waterdown each have their own downtown neighbourhoods; all walkable communities with many amenities at hand. Each downtown has a distinct character, brought about by its history, situation and relationship to Hamilton itself.

New communities within the old City boundaires have emerged over the years, too. Historic neighbourhoods like Barton Village ❶, Kirkendall/Durand ❷ (Map 42) and the Waterfront ❸ offer a rich diversity of experiences and lifestyles. Some communities face challenges, including Barton Village and King East (bottom right) as suburban growth and auto mobility brought an end to linear streetcar patterns of growth by the mid 20th century (Muller, 1995).

This section highlights some of these communities for further exploration by foot, bicycle, transit or car.

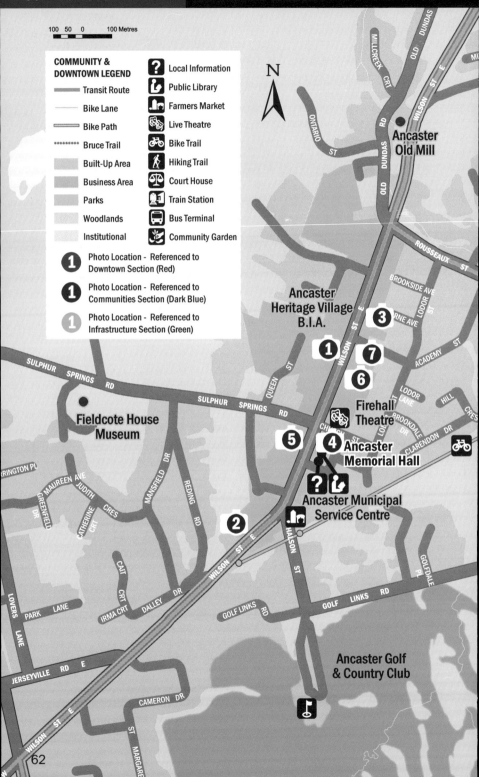

COMMUNITY & DOWNTOWN LEGEND

- Transit Route
- Bike Lane
- Bike Path
- Bruce Trail
- Built-Up Area
- Business Area
- Parks
- Woodlands
- Institutional

- ? Local Information
- Public Library
- Farmers Market
- Live Theatre
- Bike Trail
- Hiking Trail
- Court House
- Train Station
- Bus Terminal
- Community Garden

1 Photo Location - Referenced to Downtown Section (Red)

1 Photo Location - Referenced to Communities Section (Dark Blue)

1 Photo Location - Referenced to Infrastructure Section (Green)

100 50 0 100 Metres

N

Ancaster Old Mill

Ancaster Heritage Village B.I.A.

Fieldcote House Museum

Firehall Theatre

Ancaster Memorial Hall

Ancaster Municipal Service Centre

Ancaster Golf & Country Club

MILLCREEK CRT
OLD DUNDAS
WILSON ST E
ONTARIO ST
OLD DUNDAS
RD
ROUSSEAUX ST
BROOKSIDE AVE
LODOR ST
RNE AVE
ACADEMY ST
HILL
CRES
WILSON ST E
QUEEN ST
LODOR LANE
BROOKDALE DR
CLARENDON DR
GOLFDALE PL
SULPHUR SPRINGS RD
SULPHUR SPRINGS RD
CHURCH
HALSON ST
MANSFIELD DR
REDING RD
RINGTON PL
MAUREEN AVE
JUDITH
GREENFIELD DR
CATHERINE CRT
CRES
CAIT CRT
PARK LANE
LOVERS LANE
IRMA CRT
DALLEY DR
GOLF LINKS RD
GOLF LINKS RD
JERSEYVILLE RD E
CAMERON DR
WILSON ST E
ST MARGARETS
ST ANNS

62

A 19th Century Village Centre

In Ancaster's Historic Village, one could imagine horse-drawn carriages or old jalopies trundling down the street amidst the heritage buildings and low-density surroundings. The slow-paced atmosphere is a far cry from the rapidly developing Meadowlands area of Ancaster, with its car-oriented power centres. The village features a weekly farmers market, and the Firehouse Theatre.

❶ The 1971 Ancaster Township Hall is undergoing renovation and restoration.

Ancaster Village is centred on Wilson Street ❷❼, a major thoroughfare to the west end of Hamilton and Dundas. The wide boulevard and sidewalk setbacks reduce the impact of traffic, creating a comfortable, pedestrian experience.

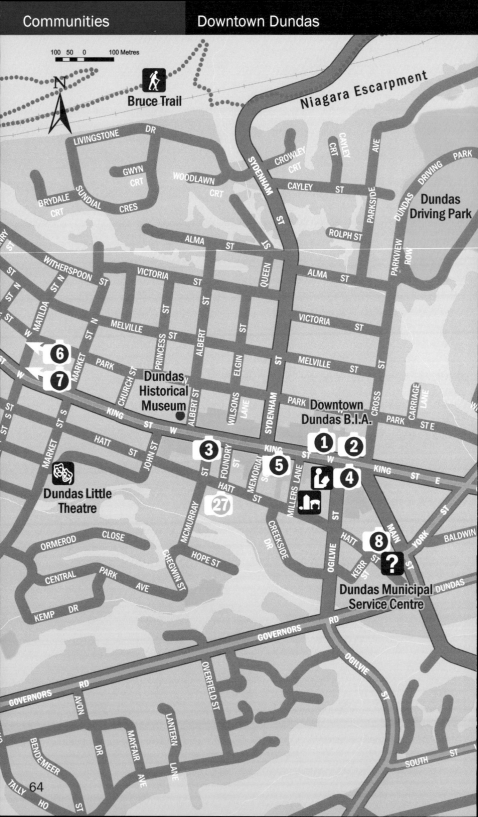

100 50 0 100 Metres

N

Bruce Trail

Niagara Escarpment

LIVINGSTONE DR
GWYN CRT
WOODLAWN CRT
BRYDALE CRT
SUNDIAL
CRES
CROWLEY CRT
CAYLEY CRT
CAYLEY ST
CAMLEY
PARKSIDE
AVE
Dundas
Driving Park
DUNDAS DRIVING PARK
ROLPH ST
PARKVIEW ROW
ALMA ST
SYDENHAM ST
QUEEN ST
ALMA ST
WITHERSPOON ST N
MATILDA ST N
VICTORIA ST
ALBERT ST
VICTORIA ST
MELVILLE ST N
PRINCESS ST
ELGIN ST
MELVILLE ST
CROSS ST
CARRIAGE LANE
PARK ST
6
7
MARKET ST N
PARK ST N
CHURCH ST N
Dundas
Historical
Museum
WILSONS LANE
SYDENHAM ST
PARK ST
Downtown
Dundas B.I.A.
PARK ST E
KING ST W
ALBERT ST
3
FOUNDRY ST
MEMORIAL SQ
KING ST W
1 **2**
5
4
KING ST E
HATT ST
JOHN ST
MCMURRAY ST
HATT ST
27
MILLERS LANE
OGILVIE ST
HATT ST
KERR ST
MAIN ST
YORK ST
BALDWIN
Dundas Little
Theatre
MARKET ST S
ORMEROD CLOSE
CENTRAL PARK AVE
KEMP DR
CHEGWIN ST
HOPE ST
CREEKSIDE DR
8
?
Dundas Municipal
Service Centre
DUNDAS
GOVERNORS RD
OGILVIE ST
GOVERNORS RD
AVON DR
OVERFIELD ST
MAYFAIR AVE
LANTERN LANE
BENDEMEER
TALLY HO
SOUTH ST

64

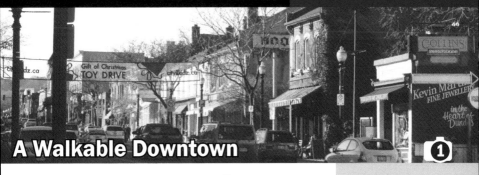

A Walkable Downtown

Dundas is known as the "Valley Town" **6** and lives in the shadow of the Niagara Escarpment and the City of Hamilton itself, yet retains a strong independent community identity. Industry was also attracted to Hatt Street, adjacent to the town centre in the early days due to water power, railway and canal to the lake. Today, some of the former industrial buildings are adapted to new uses.

3 The original Dundas Post Office is now an office and commercial building.

2 3 4 5 Heritage buildings line King Street **1**, and further along King a former high school **7** at the foot of the escarpment is being converted to residential use (bottom left). The historic Dundas Town Hall **8** is still a very active community space and municipal service centre.

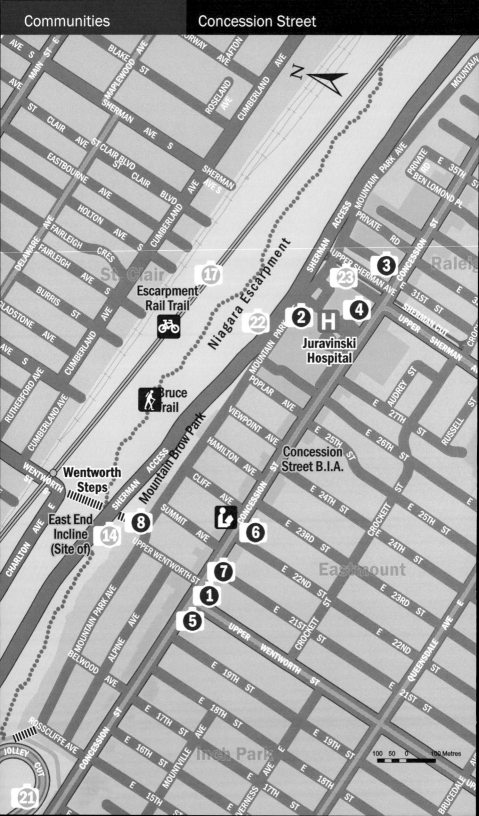

"the stuff dreams are made of"

First on the Mountain

The Movie Palace ❶ brings an appropriate sense of nostalgia to quirky Concession Street. Concession was the beachhead for development on the Mountain, becoming a more desirable place to live as access from the lower city improved. The street ❻ exemplifies the linear development pattern synonymous of its time, rather than the plazas and malls found elsewhere on the mountain.

❽ View of Wellington Street in the lower city from the site of the East End Incline ⓮ ㉒

❷❹ The Juravinski Hospital, which specializes in cancer treatment, is one of four hospitals in the Hamilton Health Sciences network (HHS, 2012), **overlooks the lower city.**

❺ The terrazzo entrance of the old Hillcrest Restaurant remains within the sidewalk at Wellington Street despite the site being redeveloped as a drug store.

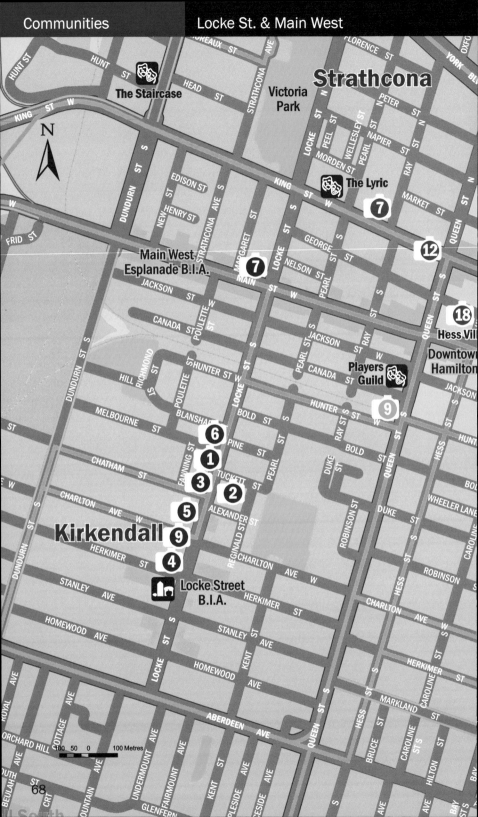

Success or hardship depends on traffic

Locke St. South between Main St. and Aberdeen Ave. is the centre of the Kirkendall neighbourhood, and has rejuvenated over the past decade as a new generation of businesses and residents move in to the area. Main St. West has yet not been so fortunate, as the five lane waves of one-way through traffic and narrow sidewalks are a stark contrast to pedestrian-friendly Locke St.

35 It is easy to tell when Locke developed as a commercial district by the dates on the buildings.

49 Creative business signs say it all.

78 The busy, one-way Main Street is a gateway to downtown from Highway 403. Do the drivers of cars travelling along at 60 km/h in narrow lanes even notice the Main West businesses and signage?

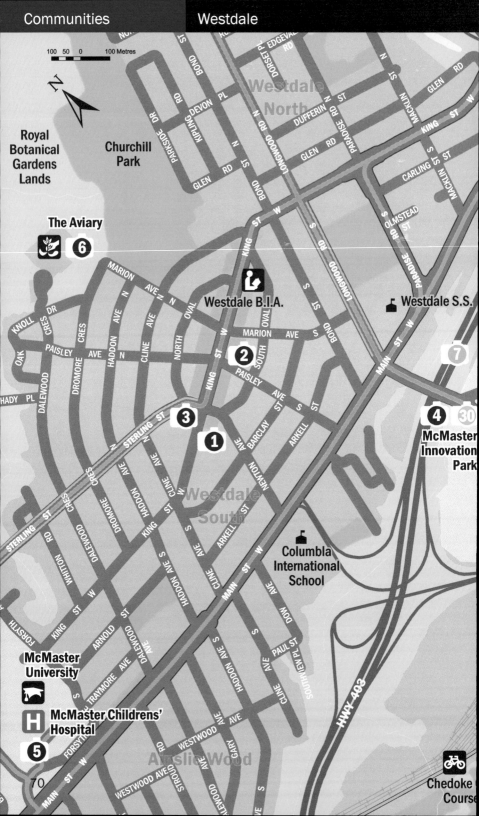

100 50 0 100 Metres

N

Royal
Botanical
Gardens
Lands

Churchill
Park

Westdale
North

The Aviary

6

Westdale B.I.A.

Westdale S.S.

7

2

3

1

4 **30**

McMaster
Innovation
Park

Westdale
South

Columbia
International
School

McMaster
University

McMaster Childrens'
Hospital

H

5

Ainslie Wood

HWY 403

Chedoke
Course

70

"Canada's first planned community"

Streets radiate out from Westdale's focal point ❷ along King Street West, between Highway 403 and McMaster University in this early 20th century planned, self-contained community originally conceptualized in 1911 and constructed over the next three decades (Horsnell, 2010). King Street used to extend through McMaster until its campus grew and the medical centre ❺ was erected in its path in the 1970s. The cul-de-sac-ing of King may have saved Westdale from the fate that the one-way streets brought to neighbourhoods east of here.

Westdale was also the end of the line for the streetcar, making it an early commuter suburb of Hamilton. The map from 1944, at bottom, shows the HSR streetcar line along King Street ending at Westdale (McFaul, 1943).

The Air photo from 1934 at the top of the page shows the early development of Westdale and McMaster University.

❷

❸

❹

❺

❶ Gateway sign to Westdale along King Street ❷❸; McMaster University influences the area with its campus, medical centre ❺, McMaster Childrens' Hospital, innovation park 4 and large student population. The Aviary ❻ and community gardens are an interesting Sunday afternoon destination.

❻

100 50 0   100 Metres

Stadium

Centre or
Barton
(formerly
Centre Mal

Ottawa Street
B.I.A.

Watermain Path
(pg. 22)

Childrens'
Museum

Gage
Park

Sewing the City's Fabric

Ottawa Street was chosen by the Canadian Institute of Planners as one of the "Great Places in Canada" in their in 2011 contest, which "celebrates special locations that people love most" (CIP, 2011). It is also the home of the first Tim Horton's. Hamilton's first shopping mall was located nearby on Barton Street ❾, but is now a big box power centre. Some of the former mall's small businesses and its farmers market ❻ relocated to Ottawa Street.

❶❷ Street art and signage reflect the area's reputation as a centre for textiles, crafts and fashion. (Photos: B. Montgomery)

❽ Gage Park is one of the largest parks in the lower city and often hosts festivals and community events.

❾ The recently completed redevelopment of Centre Mall was to include new shops along Barton Street, but the power centre developer failed to mention it would be the shops' back sides.

73

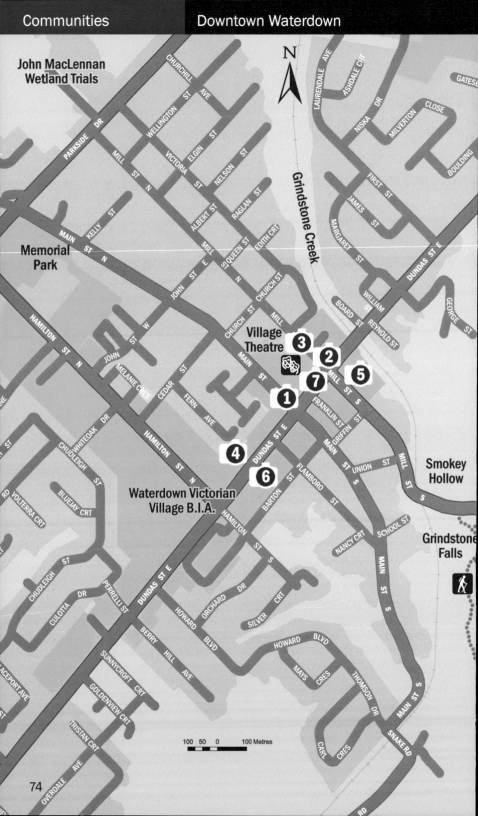

John MacLennan
Wetland Trials

Memorial
Park

Village
Theatre

Waterdown Victorian
Village B.I.A.

Smokey
Hollow

Grindstone
Falls

N

Grindstone Creek

100 50 0   100 Metres

The Victorian Village

Waterdown once boasted twelve mills along Grindstone Creek in the 1800s (Disher & Smith, 2001), so the town was aptly named. Buildings from the Victorian era ❷❸❹❺❻ line the downtown, and some of the latest developments along Dundas Street ❶ hold true to their style. Increasing suburban growth, traffic, and minimal public transit overlay modern stresses on historic charms.

❶ Dundas Street is lined by quaint shops, cafes and restaurants, but increasing traffic congestion along this route reduces its charm.

❼ Memorial Hall, home to Village Theatre Waterdown Inc, will shortly be undergoing a major facelift to improve accessibility and restore some of the building's heritage features that have been covered up over the years (O'Hara, 2012).

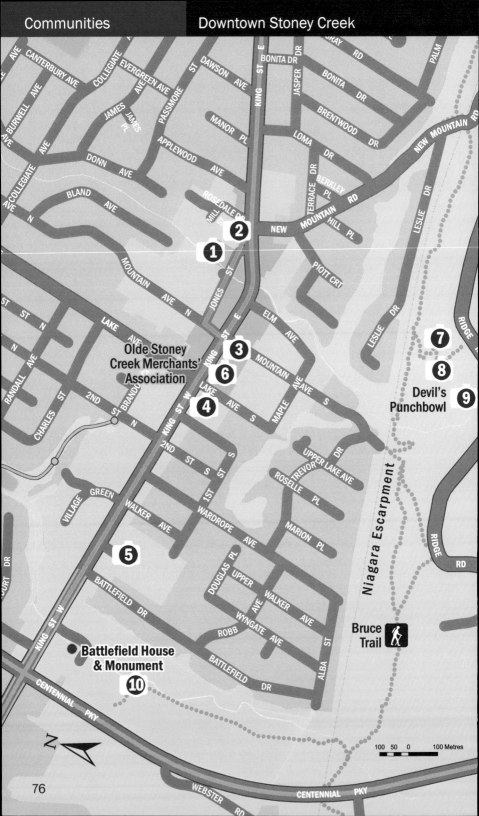

Olde Stoney Creek Merchants' Association

Devil's Punchbowl

Niagara Escarpment

Bruce Trail

Battlefield House & Monument

100 50 0   100 Metres

Stoney Creek is the site of a famous War of 1812 battle along the original road to Niagara (Evans, 1970). The Escarpment is punctuated here by the Devil's Punchbowl ❾, so named for the bowl-shape carved into the escarpment face and colourful strata of limestone. Although the businesses seem to struggle to compete with the much busier Queenston Road corridor to the north, street life is evident and this small downtown is a suburban respite.

❶ The Powerhouse 23

❿ The Battlefield Park, War of 1812 monument.

❸❹❻ A variety of buildings and streetside experiences. A new recreation centre serves the community ❺. From the escarpment, a 10 metre high illuminated cross keeps watch over Downtown Stoney Creek ❽, beside the Devil's Punchbowl waterfall and conservation area ❾. One of over 120 waterfalls in the city.

environment

The Niagara Escarpment ❶ usually comes first to mind when the environment is considered in the context of Hamilton. As this "Giant's Rib" winds its way through the urban and rural areas of the City, 126 waterfalls, of various height and intermittency, spill over its precipice, making Hamilton the "Waterfall Capital of the World" (City of Waterfalls, 2012).

Hamilton has struggled to resist a negative environmental image, brought on by its industrial past and perceived air and water quality issues. But through the hard work of a number of local actors, these issues are no longer the concern they once were. Energy recovery systems at the City's waste treatment plant ㉔ and landfills capture methane and convert it to electricity to feed into the power grid. Thanks in large part to these measures, the City has reduced its greenhouse gas output by over 16% since 2005, and is on track to meet its 2020 target of 20% (Hamilton, 2012b).

The City's Climate Change Action Charter (bottom, right) has been endorsed by over 40 public and private organizations in the city committed to positive environmental action.

But beyond the 'feel good' measures, there is still much 'heavy lifting' to be done! This section highlights conservation and environmental remediation efforts underway in the City, with particular focus on watersheds, preservation and the Harbour.

CleanAir
HAMILTON

CLIMATE CHANGE
CHAMPIONS

HAMILTON CLIMATE CHANGE ACTION CHARTER

We the undersigned agree that:

A) Scientific evidence shows climate change is happening now. There is consensus that greenhouse gases emissions caused by human activity are seriously affecting Earth's climate.

B) Climate change is having increasingly negative impacts on all of Hamilton's residents, environment and economy.

C) We need to take responsibility and act to reduce greenhouse gas emissions and prepare for climate change impacts in ways that promote economic prosperity, health and environmental benefits for all.

D) It is important for individuals and organizations to share ideas and best practices and coordinate efforts to accomplish these goals as effectively as possible.

We commit to:

Watershed Management

Four Conservation Authorities operate within the City of Hamilton to provide watershed and environmental management, as legislated by the Province of Ontario under the Conservation Authorities Act (1946). Boundaries of these authorities are based on watershed catchment areas, rather than political borders, as shown in the map below.

The Hamilton Conservation Authority (HCA) is almost completely within the City limits, while Conservation Halton, Grand River and Niagara Peninsula Conservation Authorities fill in from adjacent jurisdictions. These authorities also manage wetlands, control development within environmentally sensitive areas and operate parks throughout the City's urban and rural areas.

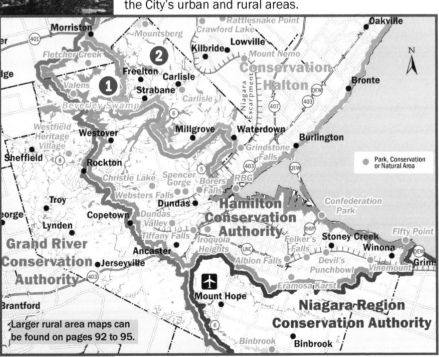

Larger rural area maps can be found on pages 92 to 95.

Environmental Preservation

Each Conservation Area park offers a unique experience to visitors, ranging from passive nature enjoyment to active recreational opportunities, including: trails, waterfalls, swimming, camping, nature interpretation, and wildlife refuges. Heritage, wildlife and cultural preservation programs are also an important environmental awareness activities available at the parks.

The Royal Botanical Gardens (RBG) is another important local organization, preserving and rehabilitating the natural environment in Cootes Paradise 83,85 and the Grindstone Creek estuary.

Topographic maps of Cootes Paradise and several Conservation Area parks are included on the next page.

The map below shows Hamilton's unique and varied physiography.

❶ **The Beverley Swamp is the third largest wetland complex in Ontario and vital to local ecology** (Curry, 2005). **The swamp is under threat from development, which could alter or contaminate the water table, and from invasive plant species phragmites (common reed), which could overwhelm native plants like cattails.**

❷ **The Raptor Centre at Mountsberg** 82.

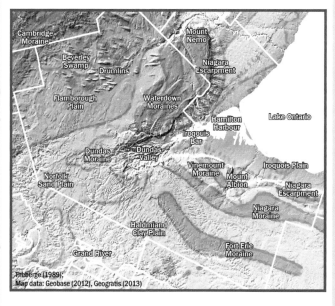

Cambridge Moraine
Beverley Swamp
Drumlins
Mount Nemo
Niagara Escarpment
Flamborough Plain
Waterdown Moraines
Hamilton Harbour
Lake Ontario
Iroquois Bar
Dundas Moraine
Dundas Valley
Vinemount Moraine
Mount Albion
Iroquois Plain
Norfolk Sand Plain
Niagara Escarpment
Niagara Moraine
Haldimand Clay Plain
Grand River
Fort Erie Moraine

Theberge (1989);
Map data: Geobase (2012), Geogratis (2013)

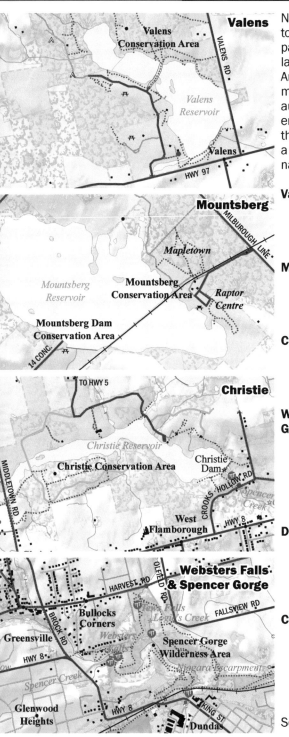

Nature and recreation come together in a sustainable partnership all over Hamilton's landscape. Several Conservation Areas are centred on reservoirs, managed by the conservation authorities to provide flood and erosion mitigation throughout their watersheds. Here are just a few of these parks and other natural recreation areas:

Valens Lake
- Camping, fishing, swimming, boat rental, wetland with boardwalk trail, birdwatching

Mountsberg
- Fishing, Raptor Centre, nature preserve, birdwatching
- Mapletown (seasonal event)

Christie Lake
- Fishing, swimming, picnics
- Trail conections to Crook's Hollow and Websters Falls.

Websters Falls and Spencer Gorge
- Hamilton's most impressive and popular waterfalls
- Trail connections to Bruce Trail, Dundas Valley and Christie

Dundas Valley
- A wildeness area right in the city with an extensive network of trails
- Historic sites and ruins

Cootes Paradise
- Managed by the Royal Botanical Gardens
- Hiking trails, birdwatching, Arboretum
- Wetland restoration

See **90** for map legend.

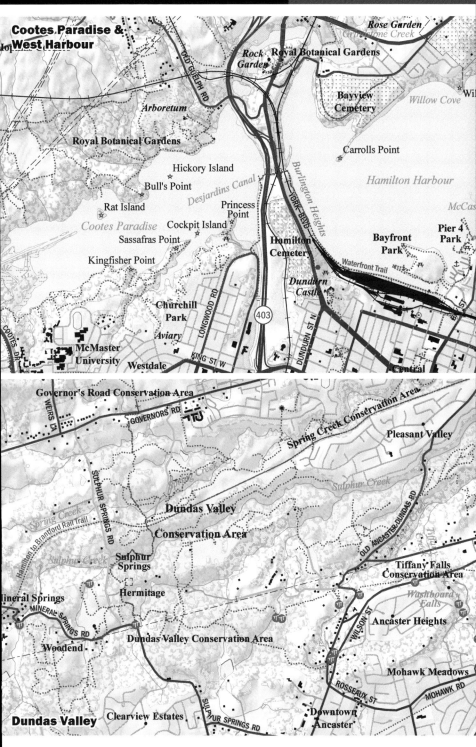

Cootes Paradise & West Harbour

Rose Garden

Griffstone Creek

Rock Garden   Royal Botanical Gardens

Arboretum

Bayview Cemetery

Willow Cove   Wil

Royal Botanical Gardens

Carrolls Point

Hickory Island

Hamilton Harbour

Bull's Point

Desjardins Canal

Burlington Heights

YORK BLVD

McCas

Rat Island

Princess Point

Cootes Paradise   Cockpit Island

Sassafras Point

Pier 4 Park

Bayfront Park

Hamilton Cemetery

Kingfisher Point

Waterfront Trail

Dundurn Castle

Churchill Park

LONGWOOD RD

403

Aviary

DUNDURN ST N

McMaster University   Westdale

KING ST W

Central

COOTES DR

Governor's Road Conservation Area

WEIRS LN

GOVERNORS RD

Spring Creek Conservation Area

Pleasant Valley

SULPHUR SPRINGS RD

Spring Creek

Sulphur Creek

Dundas Valley

Spring Creek

Hamilton to Brantford Rail Trail

Conservation Area

OLD ANCASTER-DUNDAS RD

Tiff

Sulphur Creek

Sulphur Springs

Tiffany Falls Conservation Area

ineral Springs

Hermitage

WILSON ST

Washboard Falls

MINERAL SPRINGS RD

Ancaster Heights

Dundas Valley Conservation Area

Woodend

Mohawk Meadows

Dundas Valley   Clearview Estates

SULPHUR SPRINGS RD

ROSSEAUX ST

Downtown Ancaster

MOHAWK RD

US Steel
Canada

Randle Reef

Capping a Toxic Legacy ❶

Hamilton Harbour Remedial Action Plan (RAP, 1992), identified **Randle Reef** ❶ as one of the most acutely toxic spots in the Harbour. The International Joint Commission (IJC) rated the site among the top "areas of concern" within the entire Great Lakes basin.

The Randle Reef project aims to sequester the most contaminated sediments in-situ, with "construction of a dry cap dyked containment facility about 9.5 ha (hectare) in size" (Environment Canada, 2012). The capped land will then become part of the functioning harbour port facility, and include a naturalized shoreline along the north side. Funding towards the $140 million remediation cost is being shared by all levels of government, with additional contributions from the Hamilton Port Authority and U.S. Steel (Hamilton, 2012c). Although the cost is high, an Environment Canada report estimates a total economic return of $1 billion for cleaning up the harbour, through improved environmental image, recreational and investment opportunities (Victor, 2006).

The recovery is already well underway at **Windermere Basin** where the Red Hill Creek and Hamilton's treated sewage enter the eastern end of the Harbour. Part of the basin has been filled in to restore habitat and wetlands for migratory birds (Hamilton Waterfront Trust, 2011).

❶ **Randle Reef is the nearshore area to the left of the steel factory.**

❷ **These hatchways in the middle of the Bayfront Park parking lot give a clue as to what is underneath: A combined sewer overflow tank with a capacity of 20,000 cubic metres** (Hamilton, 2005).

❸ **Bayfront Park in the West Harbour opened in 1993. Once a landfill, the park is a great success and an example of the change that can occur in less than a generation.**

Wetland Restoration (4)

Cootes Paradise **5** is a shallow lake separated from Hamilton Harbour by a sandbar called Burlington Heights. Dundas entrepreneur Peter Desjardins opened a ship canal through Cootes Paradise to Dundas in 1837, and the cut through the Heights was opened in the 1850s (Evans, 1970). This direct connection to the Harbour ultimately failed to entice more marine traffic to Dundas, as ships became too large to navigate the channel. Unfortunately, the invasive Asian Carp, a bottom-feeding fish, did enjoy the new habitat and has caused damage to the fragile wetlands surrounding Cootes Paradise 83. A barrier was installed at the mouth of the canal to keep the carp out, and gradually allow native species to recover.

Hamilton's sewers in the older parts of the city are a combined sanitary and storm water system. During periods of heavy rainfall, sewage used to be flushed out directly into the Harbour and Cootes Paradise. With the installation of six sewer overflow tanks, such as the one at **Bayfront Park** **2 3**, storm runoff can be stored temporarily until the treatment plant has the capacity to handle it (Hamilton, 2005). This key part of the RAP (1992) has resulted in significantly improved water quality in both bodies of water, enabling swimming in some parts of the harbour for the first time in decades.

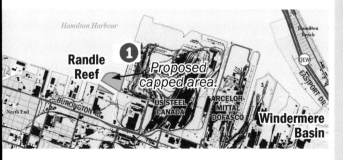

4 The Carp Barrier at the mouth of the Desjardins Canal has been effective in keeping invasive carp out of Cootes Paradise. (Photo: B. Montgomery)

5 The shore of Cootes Paradise, with its numerous shallow inlets, may be similar to the way the south shore of Hamilton Harbour was before it was infilled for industrial development.

Left: Map shows the location of projects described on this page.

rural hamilton

In the "City of Waterfalls" **79**, the many cascades can be spectacles at any time of the year **1**. The Niagara Escarpment is a defining feature of rural Hamilton, and influences different microclimates across the region suitable for a broad range of agriculture. The most fertile land is also most favoured for development, so much has been lost over the past century. The Greenbelt will help protect what is left **87**.

Quiet crossroads, like this one at Westover in Flamborough **2** often come with an old general store or schoolhouse, now used as a residences, antique shops or other small businesses.

Rural Hamilton's built and cultural heritage is preserved at Westfield Heritage Village **3**, operated by the Hamilton Conservation Authority near Rockton.

Wildlife adapts to the human-induced changes in the landscape. Great blue herons **4** are a common sight in wetlands and waterways, as are turtles, ducks, frogs, salamanders, over 380 species of bird (Curry, 2005) and large and small mammals.

Few cities can boast having caves in their backyard **5**. The Eramosa Karst is such a place, and is the newest park under the protection of the Hamilton Conservation Authority. The land was donated to the authority by the Ontario Realty Corporation after pressure to preserve this rare landscape rather than cover it with subdivisions.

This section reveals the City's rural and agricultural areas, keys to sustainability and resilience.

Greenbelt and Niagara Escarpment

Areas protected under the Niagara Escarpment and Greenbelt Plan Acts are shown on the map below. Both acts are planning policies that ensure any developments that occur in the rural and escarpment areas are in keeping with the natural character and ensuring environmental preservation. These plans, along with the legislated policies of the Conservation Authorities to protect watersheds, provide multiple layers of due diligence, but have at times been criticized for adding too much bureaucracy, cost and delay for approving even the most minor of planning permits. Environmental protection is essential to Hamilton's rural sustainability, which is under threat from the expansion of aggregate quarries, illegal dumping, and a new provincial transportation corridors (see map below).

LEGEND
Greenbelt Plan
Niagara Escarpment Plan
Urban Area
Urban Expansion Area
Niagara Escarpment
Aggregate Extraction
Proposed Quarry
NGTA Highway Corridors Proposed

Threats and Opportunities

The majority of land in Hamilton is zoned agricultural, and half of the farms are located in Flamborough (EcDev, 2008). The Hamilton Eat Local food directory is available online and in a printed map brochure from Environment Hamilton from http://www.environmenthamilton.org/eatlocal/. The local agriculture industry produces a diversity of products year-round including poultry, eggs, fruit, mushrooms, fresh produce and livestock. Sizes of operations range from small organic farms to large acreages with on-site food processing.

The horse industry is also important to rural Hamilton, and the Flamboro Downs racetrack supports a thriving local horse industry and approximately 3,000 related jobs, according to the local councillor. With the recent announcement by the Ontario Lottery Corporation that the Slots at Racetracks subsidy program will soon end, there is concern about the future of the local horse industry. Although a program will be in place to help transition the industry to a new funding model, it is likely to be an economic shift to other agricultural sectors. With the broad diversity of the agriculture and food processing industry in Hamilton, the overall outlook remains positive.

Top: Livestock farming represents a significant portion of the agricultural sector in Hamilton.

Above: The scale of agricultural enterprises ranges in size from hundreds of acres down to small community gardens and organic food co-ops.

Left: A peaceful country scene in rural Flamborough. Residents are concerned that new quarries and highways will spoil the local environment, bringing increased traffic.

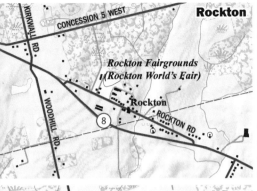

Rockton

Hamilton's rural areas seem worlds apart from the city's urban industrial core. In the 19th century, small hamlets like Rockton and Troy established to provide services to nearby farmers, such as a general store, post office, blacksmith and inn.

The agricultural heritage continues, with Rockton's Fairgrounds hosting the annual "Rockton World's Fair" fall festival.

Rockton Airfield

Nearby, Hamilton's other airport, the Rockton Airfield, is the polar opposite of Hamilton International Airport. Rockton Airfield's runways are paved with grass, and most of the planes don't even have engines! This airfield is home to one of Canada's largest gliding clubs, SOSA. Introductory flights are offered for those interested in the greenest form of flying.

Troy

Rural areas throughout Southern Ontario face development pressures from nearby urban areas. Most of Hamilton's countryside is protected by The Greenbelt, but certain areas are designated for urban expansion.

Hamlets, like Lynden, offer a quieter pace of life than living in the city's urban areas, making them popular with commuters.

Lynden

Topographic Map Legend

⊕	Waterfall		Built-up Area
▪	Building		Industrial Park
⩕	Campground		Parks
⚓	Marina		Golf Course
⋔	Picnic Area		Fairgrounds
┼┼	Railway		Quarry
▪━▪━	Municipal Boundary		Cemetery
········	Trail		Orchard
─ ─	Powerline		Vineyard
━━	Paved Road		Wooded Area
──	Unpaved Road		Wetland
──	Road built after 1990		Conservation Lands

Map data: Geobase (2012), Geogratis (2013), Queen's Printer for Ontario (2012)

Binbrook was a rural crossroads in 1990, but is now home to hundreds of new households in suburban subdivisions. Although the agricultural fairgrounds are still present, the area is now completely surrounded. With development comes pressure from new residents for city services, such as public transit.

In Winona, new and infill development encroaches on the country's most productive tender fruit agricultural zone. The QEW corridor provides convenience for commuters, draws industrial expansion, and new shopping centres to the area.

Refer to the rural maps on 92-95 for the locations of these hamlets and other features of Hamilton's rural areas.

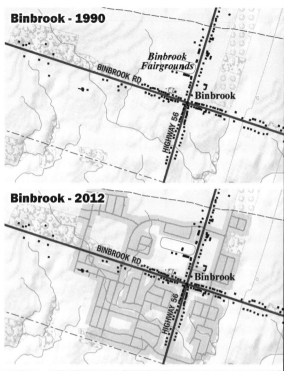

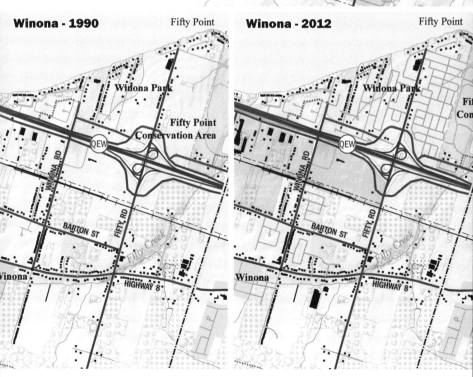

N

WELLINGTON 32 RD

WELLINGTON 34 RD

WELLINGTON 35 RD

HWY 401

HWY 6

Guelph

HWY 401

401

Morriston

WELLINGTON

Crieff

HWY 6

CA

GORE RD

6

TOWNLINE RD

REG RD 97

AVENUE RD

CLYDE RD

Clyde

COOPER RD

REG RD 97

Valens CA

Valens

Lafarge Trail

Cambridge

OLD BEVERLY RD

KIRKWALL RD

Beverley Swamp

MAIN ST

WATERLOO

SAFARI RD

MYERS RD

DUNDAS ST S

8

Sheffield

Westover

Fla m

WESTOVER RD

Branchton

BRANCHTON RD

SHEFFIELD RD

Rockton
Airfield

HWY 8

Westfield
Heritage
Village

Rockton

8

HWY 8

Christie L

WOODHILL RD

Peters Corners

HWY 52

HWY 5 W

Troy

LYNDEN RD

Orkney

BRANT RD

HWY 5

St. George

Copetown

Harrisburg

Lynden

GOVERNORS RD

POWERLINE RD

Hamilton to Brantford Rail Tr

BRANT

GOVERNORS RD E

An ca

COUNTY

4

92

POWERLINE RD

INDIAN TRAIL

Jerseyville

Brantford

WILS

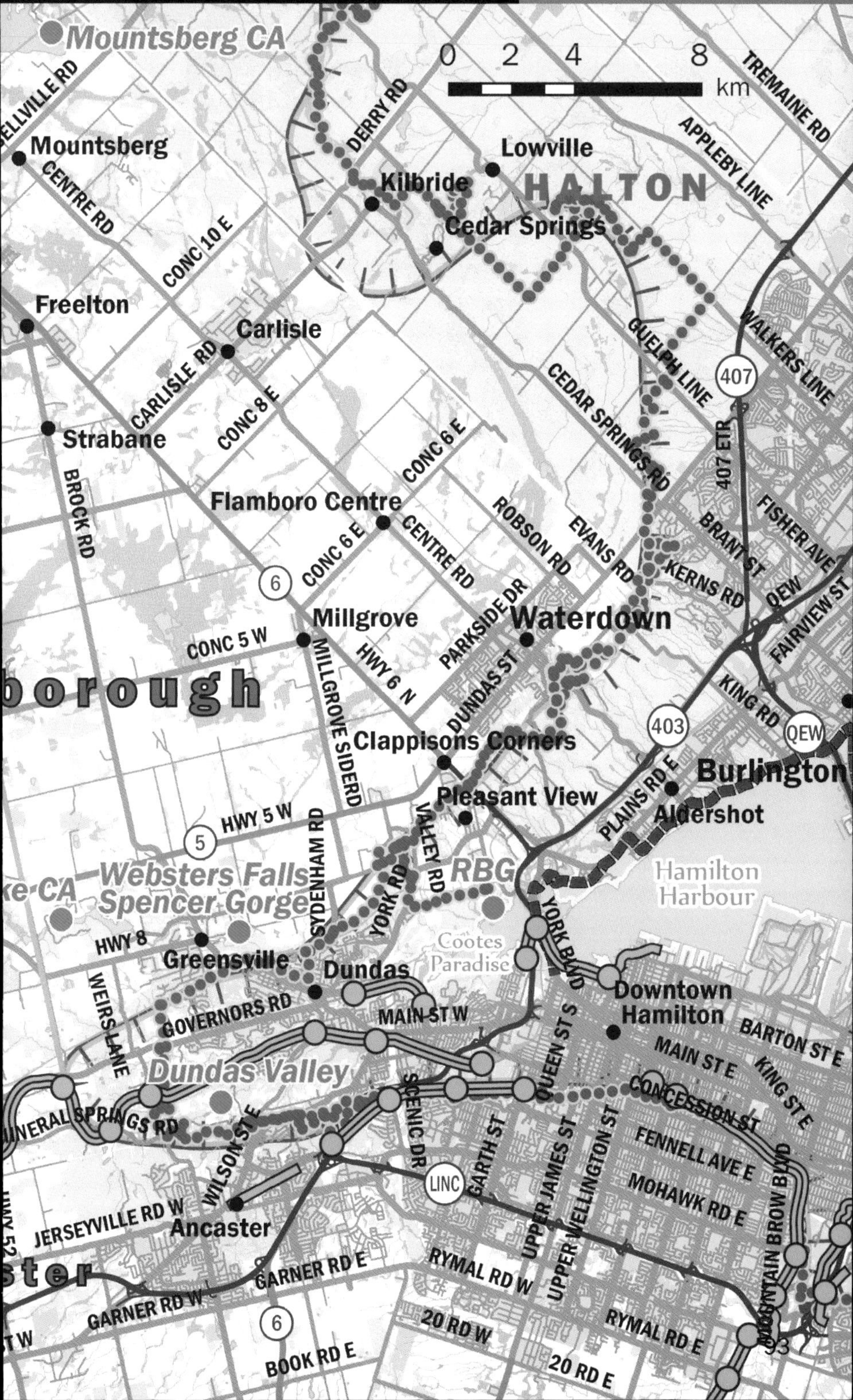

Map legend and labels:

0 2 4 8 km

HALTON

Mountsberg CA

Mountsberg
Kilbride
Lowville
Cedar Springs
Freelton
Carlisle
Strabane
Flamboro Centre
Millgrove
Waterdown
borough
Clappisons Corners
Pleasant View
Aldershot
Burlington
Websters Falls
Spencer Gorge
RBG
Hamilton Harbour
e CA
Greensville
Dundas
Cootes Paradise
Downtown Hamilton
Dundas Valley
NERAL SPRINGS RD
Ancaster
ster

Road labels:
ELLVILLE RD, CENTRE RD, CONC 10 E, DERRY RD, TREMAINE RD, APPLEBY LINE, WALKERS LINE, CARLISLE RD, CONC 8 E, GUELPH LINE, CEDAR SPRINGS RD, 407, BROCK RD, CONC 6 E, CENTRE RD, ROBSON RD, EVANS RD, KERNS RD, 407 ETR, BRANT ST, FISHER AVE, QEW, FAIRVIEW ST, CONC 6 E, 6, PARKSIDE DR, DUNDAS ST, 403, KING RD, QEW, CONC 5 W, MILLGROVE SIDERD, HWY 6 N, PLAINS RD E, HWY 5 W, 5, SYDENHAM RD, YORK RD, VALLEY RD, YORK BLVD, HWY 8, WEIRS LANE, GOVERNORS RD, MAIN ST W, BARTON ST, QUEEN ST, MAIN ST E, KING ST E, JERSEYVILLE RD W, WILSON ST E, SCENIC DR, BARTH ST, CONCESSION ST, FENNELL AVE E, UPPER JAMES ST, UPPER WELLINGTON ST, MOHAWK RD E, LINC, MOUNTAIN BROW BLVD, HWY 52, GARNER RD E, GARNER RD W, RYMAL RD W, 6, BOOK RD E, 20 RD W, 20 RD E, RYMAL RD E, 93

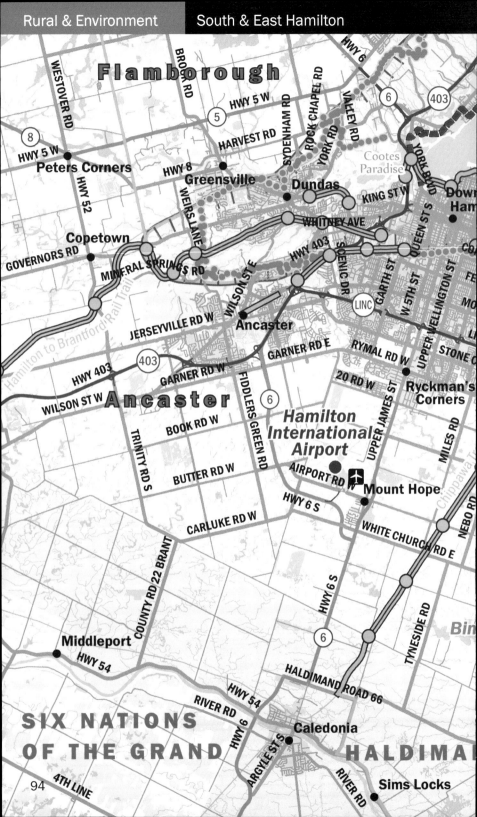

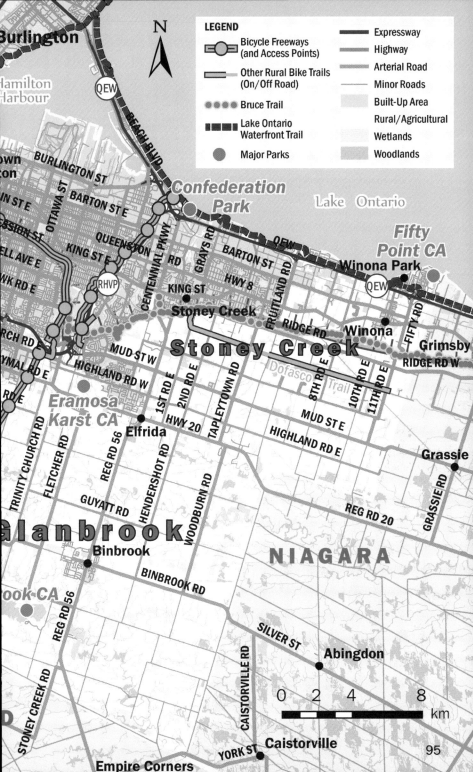

LEGEND

⊙ Bicycle Freeways (and Access Points)

▭ Other Rural Bike Trails (On/Off Road)

●●●● Bruce Trail

▰▰▰▰ Lake Ontario Waterfront Trail

● Major Parks

━━ Expressway

━━ Highway

━━ Arterial Road

── Minor Roads

Built-Up Area

Rural/Agricultural

Wetlands

Woodlands

N

Burlington

Hamilton Harbour

QEW

BEACH BLVD

BURLINGTON ST

BURLINGTON ST

OTTAWA ST

BARTON ST E

QUEENSTON RD

KING ST E

RHVP

CENTENNIAL PKWY

KING ST

Stoney Creek

GRAYS RD

Confederation Park

Lake Ontario

BARTON ST E

HWY 8

QEW

FRUITLAND RD

RIDGE RD

Fifty Point CA

Winona Park

QEW

Winona

FIFTY RD

Grimsby

RIDGE RD W

Stoney Creek

MUD ST W

HIGHLAND RD W

Eramosa Karst CA

REG RD 56

FLETCHER RD

TRINITY CHURCH RD

1ST RD E

2ND RD E

HENDERSHOT RD

Elfrida

HWY 20

TAPLEYTOWN RD

Dofasco   Trail

8TH RD E

10TH RD E

11TH RD E

MUD ST E

HIGHLAND RD E

WOODBURN RD

Grassie

GRASSIE RD

Glanbrook

Binbrook

GUYATT RD

BINBROOK RD

REG RD 20

NIAGARA

ook-CA

REG RD 56

STONEY CREEK RD

SILVER ST

CAISTORVILLE RD

Abingdon

0   2   4   8

km

Caistorville

YORK ST

95

Empire Corners

Conclusion

Symbols of resiliency are important to a community, to foster pride and generate the willingness to move forward. But, the resilience story for Hamilton does not end through symbolic change, only through continuous substantive change from within.

One of the goals of producing this book is to demonstrate the cohesive way Hamilton functions with its amalgamated suburban and rural municipalities. Judging whether the book has achieved this goal, or contributed towards a better understanding of this relationship, will be left to the reader.

For the city as a whole, it is important to raise awareness of the differences between the communities that make up the amalgamated city. The attitude that the urban core is poor and the suburbs are rich is a common one, yet increasingly inaccurate. However, the economic, cultural and demographic make-up of the urban core, suburban and rural areas are different, and this situation leads to conflicting community needs and priorities.

Ultimately, a new form of governance is needed to address such issues. It is not possible for a single municipal council to represent such diverse interests. Maintaining this diversity is essential to keeping the city's economy and resilience strong in an increasingly competitive and challenging era of technology, climate change, environmental preservation and fiscal restraint.

Another goal of this project is to strengthen local sustainability and responsibility by promoting local travel and consumption choices as well.

"Many cities have more natural features to offer than might be obvious to the visitor or even resident. Making urban green tourism information available can meet their needs for nature and green space in the city and provide new packaging alternatives and ways of profiling the city." Gibson, et al (2003)

Urban green tourism supports the city's long-term ecological health by promoting walking, cycling, and public transportation; promotes sustainable local economic and community development and vitality; celebrates local heritage and the arts; is accessible and equitable to all. Cities and regions around the world are recognizing sustainable travel and its potential for local economic development spinoffs.

Urban green tourism does not stop at the urban boundary. There are clear connections between Hamilton's urban core and the surrounding suburban rural and natural environments. Hamilton, as a region-wide city, encompasses this diversity of environmental experiences within its city limits, extending from the intensive heavy industry along the city's waterfront to the serene beauty of its remote agricultural pastures and forests.

The goals of urban green tourism also promote improved quality of life. In the case of Hamilton, downtown neighbourhoods that suffer from low esteem can benefit by having the unique aspects of these areas promoted through things as seemingly innocuous as an old building.

Hamilton: Brutal Beauty | Hidden Heritage is a step in a collective learning process needed to achieve these objectives. A much needed sense of place and identity is still lacking 12 years after Hamilton's amalgamation. A unified "brand" for the city that its residents can take pride in.

Environmental cognition and perception—gaining knowledge and sense of one's surroundings—are shaped initially by prejudice. Through collective learning, attitudes can change as people become more familiar with the place and share their knowledge and perceptions with others. But the image presented must be realistic. No place is perfect and without problems, which is why this book has presented a balanced view of the city, flaws and all. For beauty is also seen in imperfection.

The Hamilton Book is not intended to replicate the information contained in the other Hamilton tourism or economic development publications. It is not necessary to detail traditional tourism attractions like Dundurn Castle or The African Lion Safari, list accommodations, shopping or events, as this information is already appropriately promoted. Instead, your attention has been drawn to alternative features and understanding of urban green tourism in the city by:

- Connecting urban and natural environments like the Niagara Escarpment, Waterfront, Conservation Areas, rural nature preserves and agriculture.
- Promoting sustainable infrastructure and transportation, such as bicycle freeways and history of rail transport.
- Explorating urban neighbourhoods, walkable streets and built heritage.
- Discovering environmental remediation, adaptation and urban revitalization projects.
- Alternatives to traditional ways of thinking about tourism.

This book thereby makes its contribution alongside the city's other marketing efforts, and collectively strengthens the place cognition and perception in the various communities that comprise the city. These outcomes then contribute to building community identity and branding, and drive local economic development

Post-industrial cities are a relatively new phenomenon. The field of urban, green, sustainable tourism is also relatively new, as are the community planning ideologies behind resilience and renewal. Places need to differentiate themselves from one another, promote their unique strengths, and not be afraid to show imperfections as real, livable communities in order to stay relevant, resilient, and competitive in a continually changing global economy and environmental climate. This book will make at least a small contribution to connecting people with Hamilton, and increase awareness of how resilient this city can be.

Ian Dunlop, 2013

Arnott, K., Ross, M., and MacDonald, C. (2008). Hamilton book of everything. Lunenburg: Macintyre Purcell Publishing Inc.

Best, J. C. (1991). Thomas Baker McQuesten: Public works, politics and imagination. Hamilton: Corinth Press.

Blackstone Corp. (1996). Developing an urban ecotourism strategy for Metro Toronto: A feasibility assessment for the Green Tourism Partnership. Blackstone Corporation. Toronto, ON.

Brown, J. & Burns, G. (Directors). (2006). [Interview with Mark Kingwell, Professor of Philosophy, University of Toronto]. Radiant City [Motion Picture]. Canada: Burns Film Ltd., NFB, CBC

Buist, S. (2010). Code Red (Series). Hamilton, ON: The Hamilton Spectator. April 10, 2010.

Canada, Gov't. of. (1934). Air photo series A4871, 1934-11-03. Dept. of Energy, Mines and Resources.

Canadian Register of Historic Places (2012). Victoria Hall National Historic Site of Canada. Retrieved from: http://www.historicplaces.ca/en/rep-reg/place-lieu.aspx?id=2210

Canter, D. (1977). The psychology of place. London: Architectural Press.

Chapman, J. (2012). Will Hamilton's Tivoli rise again? Canadian Broadcasting Corporation. CBC News. November 6, 2012. Retrieved from: http://www.cbc.ca/hamilton/news/story/2012/11/05/hamilton-tivoli.html

Clark and Company. (1882). Map of the City of Hamilton engraved expressly for the Canadian Almanac for 1882. Toronto: Clark & Co.

CUTA. (2011). Canadian Transit Fact Book - 2010 operating data. Toronto, ON: Canadian Urban Transit Assoc.

Department of Energy, Mines and Resources (1934). Air photo series A4866. Ottawa.

Di Cicco, P. G. (2007). Municipal mind: manifestos for the creative city. Toronto: Mansfield Press

Disher, J. W. and Smith, E. A. W. (2001). By design: The role of the engineer in the history of the Hamilton Burlington area. Hamilton, ON: Hamilton Engineering Interface Inc.

Environment Canada (2012). Randle Reef sediment remediation - Hamilton Harbour. Environment Canada's role as a responsible authority. Environment Canada. Retrieved from: http://www.on.ec.gc.ca/laws/epad/responsible_authority_e.html

Evans, G. (2005). Prints of the steel city: A nostalgic view of Hamilton. Burlington: North Shore Publishing.

Evans, G. (2010). Memories of Wentworth. Burlington: North Shore Publishing.

Evans, L. (1970). Hamilton: The story of a city. Toronto: Ryerson Press

Florida, R., Mellander, C. & Stolarick, K., (2009). Talent, technology & tolerance in canadian regional development. Toronto: Martin Prosperity Institute.

Freeman, B. and Hewitt, M. (1979). Their town: The mafia, the media and the party machine. Toronto: James Lorimer & Company Publishers.

Gibson, A., Dodds, R., Joppe, M., and Jamieson, B. (2003). Ecotourism in the city? Toronto's green tourism association. International Journal of Contemporary Hospitality Management, 15(6), 324-327.

Gilbert, R. (2006). Hamilton: The electric city. Hamilton, ON: Report

Gratz, R. B. and Mintz, N. (1998). Cities back from the edge: New life for downtown. Toronto: John Wiley & Sons. Preservation Press.

Hamilton, City of. (2005). Storm water management overview. Hamilton Public Works.

Hamilton, City of. (2009a). Light Rail Technology Overview & Analysis. Hamilton, City of: Report, April 2009.

Hamilton, City of. (2009b). City hall renovation overview. Hamilton Public Works. Retrieved from: http://www.hamilton.ca/ProjectsInitiatives/CityHallRenovations/overview.htm

Hamilton, City of. (2010a). Hamilton Street Railway Operational Review. Hamilton Public Works: Final Report, May 2010.

Hamilton, City of. (2010b). Hamilton economic development strategy 2010-2015. Hamilton Planning and Economic Development Dept.

Hamilton, City of. (2010c). Celebrating 150 years of municipal drinking water. Hamilton Public Works.

Hamilton, City of. (2011a). Green roofs and living walls. Office of Energy Initiatives. Staff report to General Issues Committee. August 13, 2012.

Hamilton, City of. (2011b). Bike routes, trails & parks. Map.

Hamilton, City of. (2011c), King and Dundurn Street Design Charrette. Hamilton, City of: Report. Planning and Economic Development . B-Line Corridor Land Use Study. Retrieved from: http://www.hamilton.ca

Hamilton, City of. (2012a). Letter of understanding with the Hamilton Port Authority regarding piers 7 and 8. City

Manager's Office. Staff report to General Issues Committee. August 13, 2012.

Hamilton, City of (2012b). Clean Air Hamilton 2012 progress report. Public Health Services. Health Protection Division. Report to Board of Health. July 11, 2012.

Hamilton Civic Museums ().

Hamilton Health Sciences (HHS) (2011). McMaster University Medical Centre: the early years. Insider: The bimonthly newsletter of Hamilton Health Sciences. Vol. 9, Number 2. March, 2011.

Hamilton International Airport (HIA) (2011). 2011 Annual report. John C. Munro Hamilton International Airport.

Hamilton Waterfront Trust (2011). Windermere Basin. Hamilton Waterfront Trust. Retrieved from: http://www.hamiltonwaterfront.com/2011/11/01/windemere-basin/

Horsnell, M. J. A. (2010).Westdale: Canada's first planned community. Neighbourhood news & views. Spring 2010. Retrieved from: http://media.awwca.ca/site_media/uploads/essays/westdale_canadas_first_planned_community.pdf

HSR (2012). HSR 2012 transit guide. (Map). Hamilton Public Works. The Hamilton Street Railway.

Jacobs, A. J. (2009). The impacts of variations in development context on employment growth : a comparison of central cities in Michigan and Ontario, 1980-2006. Economic development quarterly. 23(4) 351-371.

Land Information Ontario (LIO). (2011). Ontario Road Network. Ministry of Natural Resources. Queens Printer for Ontario.

MacLeod, M. (2011). Big plans loom at old knitting mill. Hamilton Spectator. Thurs., June 30, 2011. Retrieved from: http://www.thespec.com/news/business/article/555633--big-plans-loom-at-old-knitting-mill

Manson, B. (2002) Getting around Hamilton: a brief history of transportation in and around Hamilton, 1750 to 1950. North Shore Publishing: Burlington, ON.

Manson, B. (2012a). Lister Block. Historical Hamilton. Retrieved from: http://historicalhamilton.com/beasley/lister-block/

Manson, B. (2012b). LIUNA Station. Retrieved from http://historicalhamilton.com/beasley/liuna-station/

McFaul, W. L. (1943). Map of City of Hamilton, Ontario. City of Hamilton. Engineers Office 1943.

McGreal, R. (2011). Making amalgamation work for Hamilton. Raise the hammer. Blog entry. Sept. 9, 2011. Retrieved from: http://raisethehammer.org/article/1458/making_amalgamation_work_for_hamilton

Metrolinx. (2008). The Big Move: Transforming transportation in the Greater Toronto and Hamilton Area. Toronto: Greater Toronto Transportation Authority.

Milner, A., (2009). Hamilton Street Railway–The World's first CNG transit fleet. Interview. Canadian Natural Gas Vehicle Alliance. Accessed from: http://www.cngva.org

Muller, P. O. (1995). Transportation and urban form: Stages in the spatial evolution of the American metropolis. The geography of urban transportation. Guilford Press. Hanson, S. (Ed.)

Noble, K., Nicol, J. and Fine, P. (1999). Eaton's goes bankrupt. The canadian encyclopedia. Historica Dominion Institute. Retrieved from: http://www.thecanadianencyclopedia.com/articles/macleans/eatons-goes-bankrupt

O'Hara, C. (2012). Upgrades in the works for Waterdown hall. Flamborough Review. Tuesday, August 21, 2012. Retrieved from: http://www.flamboroughreview.com/news/upgrades- in- the- works- for- waterdown- hall/

Proulx, D. (1971). Pardon my lunchbucket. Hamilton, City of.

Remedial Action Plan (1992). Remedial Action Plan Hamilton Harbour Stage I Report: Environmental conditionds and problem definition. Canada-Ontario agreement respecting Great Lakes Water Quality.

Renew Hamilton. (2012). Trebble Hall. Hamilton Chamber of Commerce. Retrieved from http://renewhamilton.ca/portfolio/treble-hall

Rybczynski, W. (1995). City life: urban expectations in a new world. New York: Scribner.

Spectator, The (2007). Redhill by the numbers. Hamilton Spectator. November 16, 2007. Retrieved from: http://www.thespec.com/Local/article/282577

Stamp, R. M. (1987). QEW Canada's first superhighway. Erin, ON: Boston Mills Press.

Statistics Canada. (2012a). Hamilton, Ontario (Code 3525005) and Hamilton, Ontario (Code 3525) (table). Census Profile. 2011 Census. Statistics Canada Catalogue no. 98-316-XWE. Ottawa. Released October 24, 2012. http://www12.statcan.gc.ca/census-recensement/2011/dp-pd/prof/index.cfm?Lang=E (accessed October 30, 2012).

Statistics Canada. (2012b). Hamilton, Ontario (Code 3525005) and Ontario (Code 35) (table). Census Profile. 2011 Census. Statistics Canada Catalogue no. 98-316-XWE. Ottawa. Released October 24, 2012.

Statistics Canada. (2012c). GeoSearch. 2011 Census. Statistics Canada Catalogue no. 92-142-XWE. Ottawa, Ontario. Data updated October 24, 2012. http://geodepot.statcan.gc.ca/GeoSearch2011-GeoRecherche2011/GeoSearch2011-GeoRecherche2011.jsp?lang=E&otherLang=F

Theberge, J. B. (Ed.) (1989). Legacy: The natural history of Ontario. Toronto. McClelland & Stewart.

Tumber, C. (2012). Small, gritty and green: The promise of America's smaller industrial cities in a low-carbon world. Cambridge, MA: MIT Press.

Turkstra, H. (2012). Herman Turkstra on the Board of Ed building. The Hamiltonian (Blog). Retrieved from: http://www.thehamiltonian.net/2012/02/herman-turkstra-on-board-of-ed-building.html

Van Dongen, M. (2011). Sherman access ready to roll Monday. Hamilton Spectator. Saturday, October 29, 2011. Retrieved from: http://www.thespec.com/news/local/article/616785--sherman-access-ready-to-roll-monday

Van Dongen, M. (2012). Drop in water usage will save city millions. Hamilton Spectator. Tuesday, August 14, 2012. Retrieved from: http://www.thespec.com/news/local/article/779891--drop-in-water-usage-will-save-city-millions

Victor, P. and Hanna, E. (2006). Benefits assessment: Randle Reef sediment remediation. Environment Canada.

Wilson, P. (2012). Jackson square turns 40 and fights for a future. Canadian Broadcasting Corporation. CBC Hamilton. Retrieved from: http://www.cbc.ca/hamilton/talk/story/2012/08/13/hamilton-jackson-mall-downtown.html

Web Sources:

AGH (2012). Art Gallery of Hamilton. http://www.artgalleryofhamilton.com

Canadian Institute of Planners. (2011). Great Places in Canada. http://www.cip-icu.ca/greatplaces/en/2011_Winners/index.html

City of Waterfalls (2012) http://www.cityofwaterfalls.ca

Committee to Free Flamborough. http://www.freeflamborough.com

Environment Hamilton. http://www.environmenthamilton.org.

Fromers. Sustainable travel & ecotourism. http://www.frommers.com/destinations/newyorkcity/0021020277.html (Accessed November, 2011).

Hamilton, City of, Teranet Inc. (2012). http://map.hamilton.ca/interactivemaps/framesetup.asp

Hamilton Civic Museums. http://www.hamilton.ca/CultureandRecreation/Arts_Culture_And_Museums/HamiltonCivicMuseums/

Hamilton Conservation Authority. http://www.conservationhamilton.ca

Hamilton: The city of waterfalls. http://cityofwaterfalls.ca/ (Accessed December 10, 2011)

Hamilton Public Library (HPL) (2012). Historical Images. Retrieved from http://www.hpl.ca/local-history/historical-images

Geobase. http://www.geobase.ca

Geogratis. http://geogratis.cgdi.gc.ca/geogratis/en/index.html

Green Map System, Inc. (2012). http://www.greenmap.org/ (Accessed December 10, 2011)

The International Ecotourism Society (TIES). What is ecotourism? http://www.ecotourism.org/site/c.orLQKXPCLmF/b.4835303/k.BEB9/What_is_Ecotourism__The_International_Ecotourism_Society.htm (Accessed November, 2011).

The Lister Block. http://www.thespeczone.ca/James_Project/Second_Lister.html (Accessed Dec. 10, 2011)

MSA (2012). McCallum Sather Architects. http://www.msarch.ca

NGTA (2012). Niagara to GTA corridor and environmental assessment study. (Website) Retrieved from: http://www.niagara-gta.com/

Parrish and Heimbecker (2012). http://www.parrish-heimbecker.com

Raise the Hammer. http://www.raisethehammer.org

Renew Hamilton. http://www.renewhamilton.ca

Tourism Hamilton. http://www.tourismhamilton.com

Urbanicity. http://www.urbanicity.ca

Links to more resources and information at:

http://www.hamiltour.ca/links

Like Hamilton: Brutal Beauty- Hidden Heritage, and join the discussion on Facebook!

Index

CPSIA information can be obtained at www.ICGtesting.com
Printed in the USA
LVIW01n0057260117
521965LV00001B/1